NATIONAL GEOGRAPHIC

OUR WORLD

STUDENT BOOK 5

Series Editors
JoAnn (Jodi) Crandall
Joan Kang Shin

Author
Ronald Scro

NATIONAL GEOGRAPHIC LEARNING | CENGAGE Learning®

Australia • Brazil • Japan • Korea • Mexico • Singapore • Spain • United Kingdom • United States

NATIONAL GEOGRAPHIC

OUR WORLD

Let's sing! TR: B41

This is our world.
Everybody's got a song to sing.
Each boy and girl.
This is our world!

I say "our," you say "world."
Our!
World!
Our!
World!

I say "boy," you say "girl."
Boy!
Girl!
Boy!
Girl!

I say everybody move...
I say everybody stop...
everybody stop!

This is our world.
Everybody's got a song to sing.
Each boy and girl.
This is our world!

Unit 1 Extreme Weather 4
Unit 2 Copycat Animals 20
Unit 3 Music in Our World 36
Units 1-3 Review 52
Let's Talk
It's my turn. 54
Who's going to take notes? 55

Unit 4 Life Out There 56
Unit 5 Arts Lost and Found 72
Unit 6 Amazing Plants! 88
Units 4-6 Review 104
Let's Talk
Can I borrow your bike? 106
It could work. 107

Unit 7 Volcanoes 108
Unit 8 Reduce, Reuse, Recycle 124
Unit 9 Cool Vacations! 140
Units 7-9 Review 156
Let's Talk
No way! 158
Our presentation is about... 159

Irregular Verbs 160
Cutouts 161
Stickers

Unit 1

Extreme Weather

In this unit, I will . . .

- talk about types of extreme weather.
- describe the damage storms can cause.
- identify ways to prepare for extreme weather.
- write a personal narrative.

Check T for *True* and F for *False*.

1. The temperature is freezing cold. Ⓣ Ⓕ
2. This person is walking carefully on the ice. Ⓣ Ⓕ
3. There was a hurricane. Ⓣ Ⓕ
4. The trees are covered with ice. Ⓣ Ⓕ

Versoix, Switzerland

1 Listen and read. TR: A2

2 Listen and repeat. TR: A3

We know we can't control the weather. It can be beautiful, wild, and dangerous, often all at the same time. Scientists try to predict weather in different ways. They tell us when extreme weather is coming. Then we can try to protect ourselves.

Thunderstorms bring heavy rain with loud **thunder** and **lightning.** If too much rain falls in a short time, it can cause a **flood.** Too little rain makes the land dry and can cause a **drought.** When it's very cold, a rainstorm can turn into an **ice storm** or a **blizzard.**

a hurricane

a sandstorm

Wind is a dangerous force. In a **tropical storm,** the wind **speed** can be more than 100 kilometers (60 miles) per hour. Wind in a **hurricane,** or cyclone, is even faster.

A **tornado** is a column of wind that rotates very fast. High winds in dry places such as deserts can pick up sand and cause a **sandstorm.**

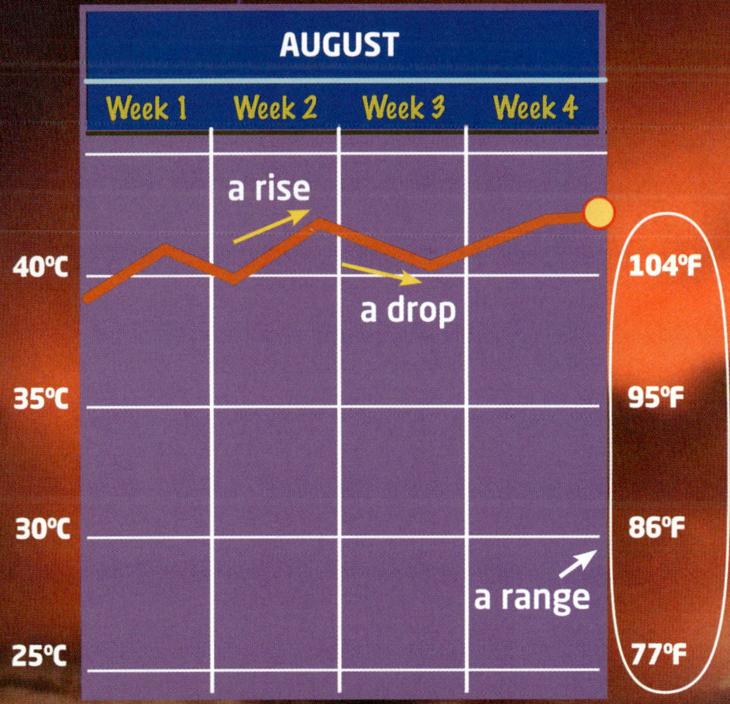

We can only live within a specific **range** of temperatures. At times, temperatures **rise** too high or **drop** too low. It not only feels bad, it can be dangerous! In a **heat wave,** the weather stays very hot for days or even weeks.

3 **Work with a partner.** What did you learn? Ask and answer.

4 Listen, read, and sing. TR: A4

Bad Weather

There's bad weather on the way!
There's bad weather on the way!

Is it going to storm? Yes, it is!
Is there going to be lightning? Yes, there is!
Is there going to be thunder? Yes, there is!

When there's going to be a storm, I hurry inside!

Be prepared for emergencies.
It's always good to be safe. You'll see!
Grab supplies and a flashlight, too.
Seek shelter. It's the safe thing to do!

Is there going to be a blizzard? Yes, there is!
Is there going to be an ice storm? Yes, there is!
Is it going to be cold? Oh, yes it is!

If there's going to be a blizzard, I hurry inside!

Be prepared for emergencies.
It's always good to be safe. You'll see!
Grab supplies and a flashlight, too.
Seek shelter. It's the safe thing to do!

Is there going to be a hurricane? Yes, there is!
Is the wind going to howl? Yes, it is!
Are the waves going to rage? Yes, they are!

If there's going to be a hurricane, we evacuate!

Be prepared for emergencies.
It's always good to be safe. You'll see!
Grab supplies and a flashlight, too.
Seek shelter. It's the safe thing to do!
Seek shelter. It's the safe thing to do!

5 **Work with a partner.** Ask and answer.

1. What bad storm in your town do you remember?
2. What did you do to prepare?
3. What did you think and feel during the storm?

GRAMMAR TR: A5

Is it **going to** rain tomorrow? No, it's **going to** snow tomorrow.
I'm **going to** listen to the weather report at 8:00.
He's **going to** put on his snow boots.

6 **Write.** What is the weather going to be like?

Sunday

Monday

Tuesday

Wednesday

Thursday

Friday

1. It's going to be sunny on Sunday.
2. ______________________________
3. ______________________________
4. ______________________________
5. ______________________________
6. ______________________________

7 **Work with a partner.** Read. Ask and answer. Take turns.

1. Why can't we go to the park tomorrow? (rain)
2. Won't she get wet walking in the rain? (take an umbrella)
3. Why is she closing the windows? (rain)
4. When will he get a new rain coat? (today)

8 **Write.** What are you going to do? Write sentences.

A thunderstorm is coming. ______________________________

____

____

____

A heat wave is coming. ______________________________

____

____

____

A hurricane is coming. ______________________________

____

____

____

9 **Work with a partner.** What about you? Talk about today and tomorrow. Ask and answer.

10 **Listen and repeat.** Then read and write. TR: A6

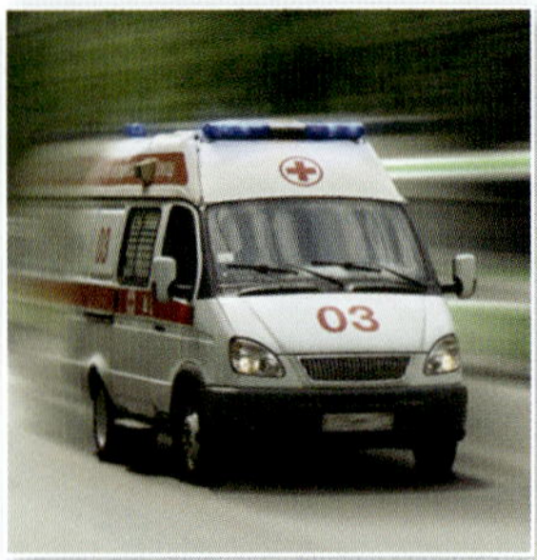

an emergency

a plan

a flashlight

supplies

evacuate

a shelter

When a weather forecaster predicts bad weather, you can make a ________________ to prepare. To protect yourself from wind and rain, you should go to a ________________. If the electricity goes off, use a ________________ to see in the dark. You can store ________________ in a safe place so that you have food to eat. A really bad storm can affect the whole town. In an ________________ like that, people have to ________________ and go where it is safer.

11 **Listen and stick.** Find out what to do next. Place your stickers in the correct order. Work with a partner. Summarize the weather report. TR: A7

A hurricane is coming. It's an emergency.

Yes, I put emergency in number 1. That's correct.

1	2	3	4	5

GRAMMAR TR: A8

If the weather **is** cold, I **put on** my winter coat.
If I **see** lightning, I **go** inside.
If a sandstorm **comes,** I **close** all the windows.

12 **Match and make logical sentences.** Then write five sentences of your own in your notebook.

I see lightning when I'm swimming	I look for a boat
it rains	I wear gloves and boots
a storm comes	I try to stay cool
the temperature rises	get out of the water
a flood comes	go inside the house
it snows	I carry an umbrella

13 **Play a game.** Cut out the cards on page 161. Play with a partner. Take turns. Match and make sentences. Keep the cards.

14 Listen and read. TR: A9

Tornado Trouble

Tornadoes happen all over the world. There's even a place called Tornado Alley. Josh Wurman studies extreme weather. He joined a team of other scientists to study tornadoes in Tornado Alley. One day, the blue sky turned black. A giant cloud came toward the team. The cloud had winds that moved in a circle. Inside his truck, Wurman watched the storm through his window and on his instruments. Colors on the computer screen showed where the rain fell and where the wind was the strongest.

The winds twisted the storm tighter and tighter into the shape of a funnel. When the funnel touched the ground, it became a tornado! The tornado looked like a giant, gray elephant's trunk. It moved one way, then another way. As the tornado moved across the ground, the team came dangerously close. They dropped special instruments close to the storm. These instruments showed wind speed, temperature, and how much rain was falling.

The tornado twisted and moved for half an hour. The team watched the storm and their instruments the whole time. Then the tornado leaned over slowly like a soft rope. Poof! It was gone. The excitement was over. But Wurman and his team have a lot more work to do. The information from their instruments will help them predict other tornadoes so that they can warn people and save lives.

weird but true It once rained frogs on a town in Serbia. A small tornado dropped them there.

15 **Work in groups of three.** Discuss and answer the questions.

1. What is the shape of a tornado?
2. Where does a funnel touch to become a tornado?
3. Why do scientists study tornadoes?
4. What do scientists use to learn about tornadoes?

16 **Work with a partner.** How does a tornado form? Match the text to each step. Discuss.

a. Warm and cold air currents twist winds into a funnel. Then the funnel touches the ground.

b. Warm air and cold air come together. They make a twisting wind of air that moves in circles.

c. The twisting air stands up. Warm air moves up. Cold air moves down.

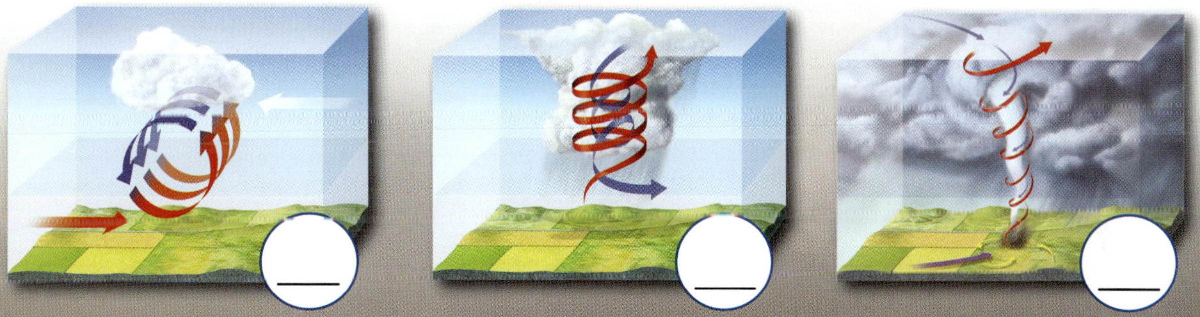

17 **Work with a group.** Compare tornadoes and hurricanes. Discuss. Complete the chart.

Tornado	Hurricane
	Origin: They form over water. Duration: They last a week.

Personal Narrative

A personal narrative tells a story. It describes something that happened. A good writer describes details using the senses—sight, sound, taste, smell, and touch. Readers should feel like they were really there. You can use words like *after, before, next,* and *then* to show the sequence of events.

18 **Read.** Read the personal narrative. How does the writer describe the hurricane? How does the writer describe what she hears and sees? How does she feel? Circle the words that relate to the senses and emotions. Underline the words and expressions that show the sequence of events.

Safe not Sorry!

Last year, the weather forecaster told us that a hurricane was coming. A hurricane is always scary, but a little exciting, too. When a hurricane comes, we know what to do. We have a family plan. First, I had to help my dad put heavy wood over the windows. It was hard work.

When the hurricane came, we could hear the strong winds outside. We could hear the rain coming down hard. Then suddenly we heard a really loud noise. And then something hit our house really hard! Everyone was worried. What could it be? After the storm, we walked outside. Part of a tree hit the wood on the window. I am so happy we covered the windows! Next time, I won't say the wood is too heavy.

19 **Write.** Write about an extreme weather experience. Give details using the senses. Help the reader feel what you felt.

20 **Work in a small group.** Share your writing.

NATIONAL GEOGRAPHIC

Mission

Understand Weather.

- Why is it important to understand weather? Work in a group. Discuss.
- How can you learn more about extreme weather?
- What do you do in dangerous weather? Write your ideas in the box.

"It all started when I was about six years old and saw that fantastic tornado in The Wizard of Oz.*"*

Tim Samaras
Severe Storm Researcher
Emerging Explorer

- Share your ideas with another group. Are they the same or different? Decide which ideas everyone thinks are best.

Storm chasers, Oklahoma, USA

21 Find out how windy it is.

1. Work in small groups to make a wind speed indicator.
2. Make an X with two pieces of cardboard. Staple it.
3. Staple one paper or plastic cup to each of the four ends.
4. Color one of the cups with a marking pen.
5. Push a push pin in the center of the X.
6. Push the pin into a pencil eraser.
7. Hold the pencil up and count the turns in one minute.

The faster the cups turn, the windier it is!

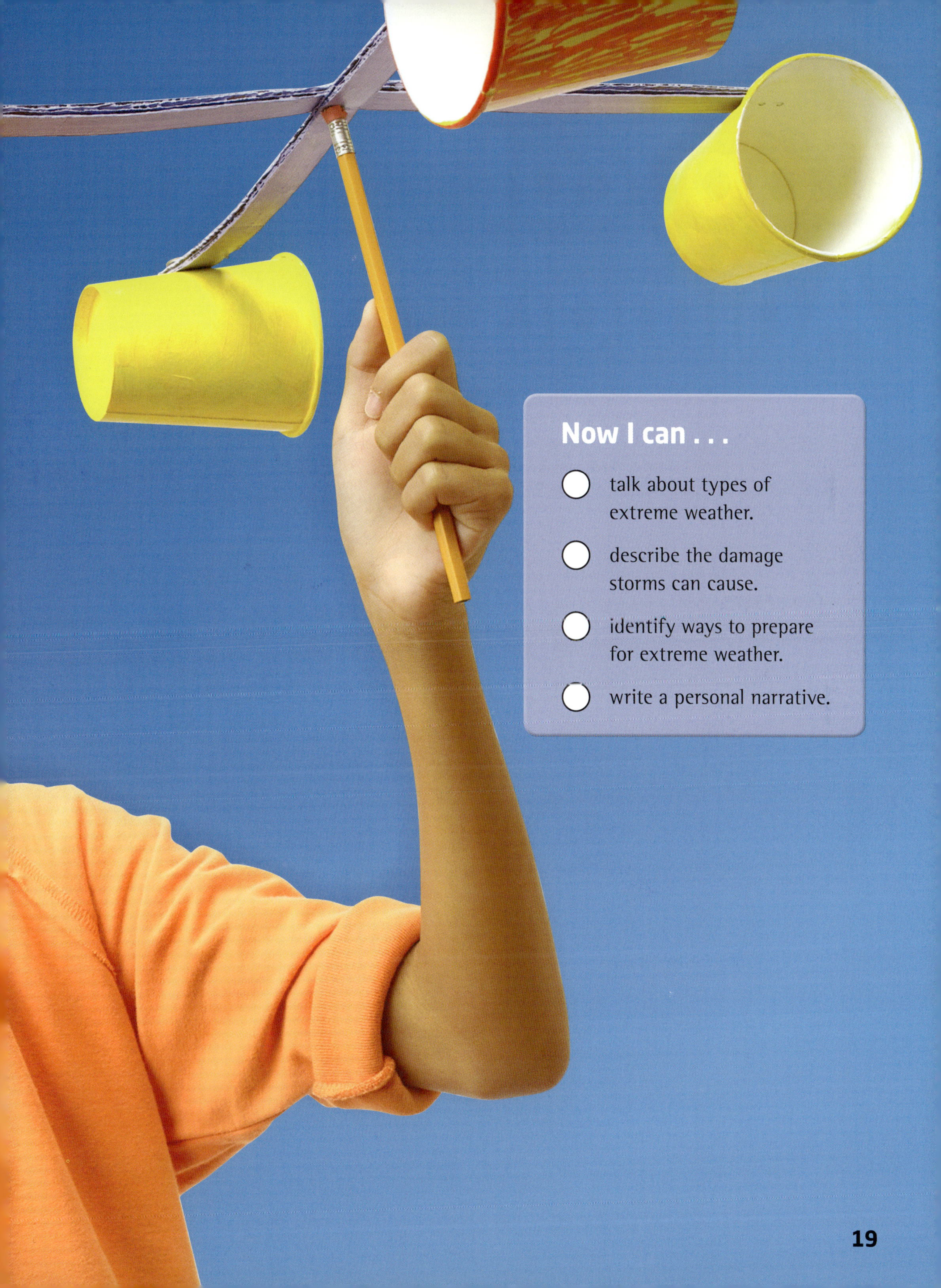

Now I can . . .

- ◯ talk about types of extreme weather.
- ◯ describe the damage storms can cause.
- ◯ identify ways to prepare for extreme weather.
- ◯ write a personal narrative.

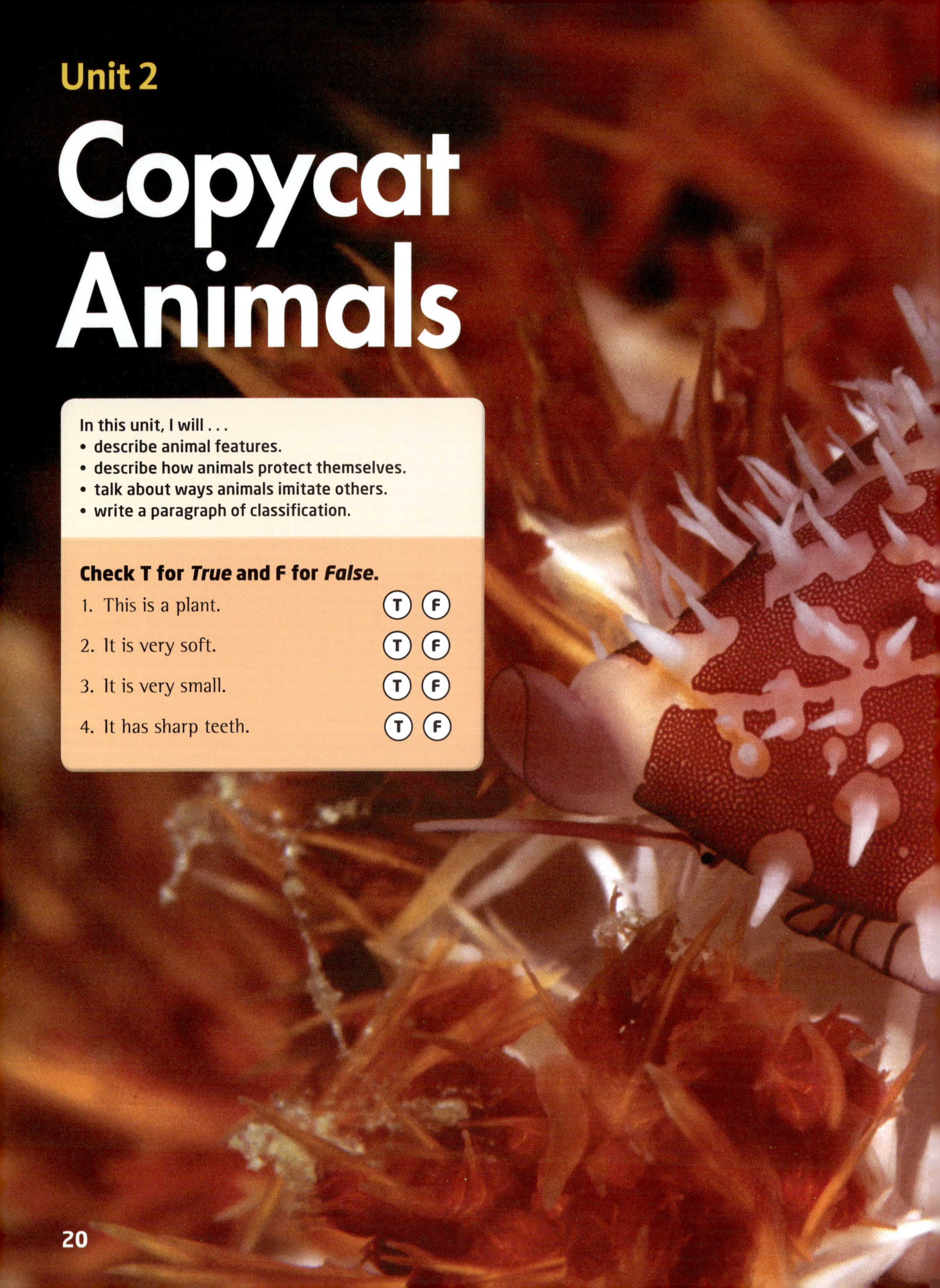

Unit 2

Copycat Animals

In this unit, I will . . .

- describe animal features.
- describe how animals protect themselves.
- talk about ways animals imitate others.
- write a paragraph of classification.

Check T for *True* and F for *False*.

1. This is a plant. (T) (F)
2. It is very soft. (T) (F)
3. It is very small. (T) (F)
4. It has sharp teeth. (T) (F)

Allied cowrie,
Papua New Guinea

1 **Listen and read.** TR: A10

2 **Listen and repeat.** TR: A11

Some animals can look like other animals or even like a plant! These copycats are trying to hide from or trick a hungry **predator.** They can look like another more dangerous animal or like another animal the predator doesn't like to eat.

This cheetah's black **spots** act as **camouflage.** This way, the cheetah doesn't **frighten** its **prey** when it's time to **hunt.**

This colorful frog has **stripes** on its skin. The bright colors tell hungry predators that the frog is **poisonous.**

These butterflies are not the same **species,** but they **resemble** each other. The top one tastes bad. The other one **copies** its shape and colors, and tastes bad, too.

This **insect** is as green as a leaf. It **imitates** the **characteristics** of color and shape of leaves to help it **hide** from predators.

3 **Work with a partner.** What did you learn? Ask and answer.

4 Listen, read, and sing. TR: A12

It's a Wild World

It's a wild world!
It's work to stay alive!
Animals do amazing things
in order to survive.

An insect that looks like a leaf
copies plants to get relief.
Predators are everywhere,
and looking for a feast!

CHORUS

Camouflage and imitate.
Resemble and escape!
Animals hide in front of our eyes, every day.

The hunter and the hunted,
predator and prey,
must hunt or hide to stay alive,
each and every day.

A pretty frog can be as deadly as a snake.
Its stripes tell its enemies
"You'd better stay away!"

CHORUS

It's a wild world!

5 Work with a partner. Ask and answer.

1. What predators have you seen?
2. What is their prey?
3. How does the prey avoid predators?

Lionfish, Indonesia

GRAMMAR TR: A13

That katydid is **as green as** the leaf it sits on.
That butterfly is not **as pretty as** the blue one.
Poison dart frogs are **as dangerous as** some snakes.

6 **Read and write.** Work with a partner. Take turns. Compare.

1. some insects / thin / sticks

____

2. a polar bear / white / snow

____

3. king snakes / not dangerous / coral snakes

____

4. a bee sting / bad / a wasp sting

____

5. a lion / not loud / a howler monkey

____

a bee

a wasp

7 **Compare the animals.** Choose one word from each group. Make sentences.

8 **Work in a group.** Take turns. Make sentences. Use the last word in each sentence to start the next sentence.

9 **Listen and repeat.** Then read and write. **TR: A14**

The butterfly fish **confuses** its predators with a spot like an eye.

The jaguar **attacks.**

The cobra **defends** itself. The mongoose **avoids** its bite.

The deer **escapes** by running away.

1. All predators ______________________ prey.
2. Bluebirds ______________________ their eggs from predators.
3. Calabar pythons have tails that look like heads. This ______________________ predators so they will not know where to strike!
4. Some animals use camouflage to ______________________ predators.
5. A rabbit that runs fast can ______________________ the coyote that chases it.

10 **Listen.** Stick *True* or *False*. Work with a partner. Compare your answers. **TR: A15**

The spot on the tail looks like an eye.
The sentence is true.

You are right! My turn.

1	2	3	4	5

GRAMMAR TR: A16

The jaguar **is** dangerous, **isn't it?**
Those snakes **are** scary, **aren't they?**
This insect **looks** like a stick, **doesn't it?**
Giraffes **don't** eat meat, **do they?**

That frog **wasn't** poisonous, **was it?**
The cat **escaped** the dog, **didn't it?**
The dogs **were** loud, **weren't they?**
The cats **weren't** friendly, **were they?**

11 **Read.** Complete the sentences.

1. The katydid is pretending it's a leaf, ______________________________?
2. The donkey doesn't look thirsty, ______________________________?
3. That python really confused its predator, ______________________________?
4. Cats like sleeping in the sun, ______________________________?
5. Baby penguins are so cute, ______________________________?
6. Those weren't copycat animals, ______________________________?

12 **Play a game.** Cut the question tags on p. 163. Glue nine to complete your game. Listen. Which tag completes the sentence? If you have it, draw an X on the square. TR: A17

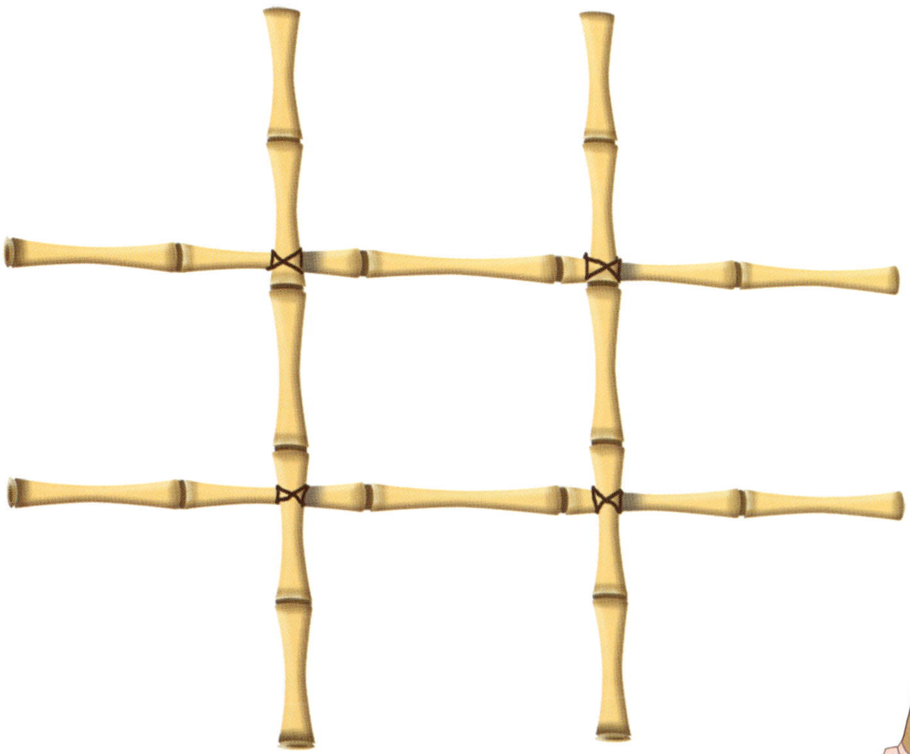

13 **Listen and read.** TR: A18

Copycats

The leafy sea dragon is a weird but beautiful copycat. From its name you would think it imitates a dragon, wouldn't you? But no, it only gets that name from its funny shape. The leafy sea dragon imitates what is around it. It lives in seaweed, and so its body looks like a seaweed leaf. The sea dragon imitates the shape and color of seaweed, and it even looks like floating seaweed when it moves. It doesn't use the parts of its body that look like a leaf to swim. It uses fins that are transparent, so it's hard to see them move.

The leafy sea dragon does not only look like a copycat. It also dances like a copycat. A male and female sea dragon will copy each other's movements for hours!

The mimic octopus is the only sea creature that can imitate many different species. It not only changes its color, it also changes its shape. It has arms as thick as pencils. When it spreads them wide, they look like the spines of a lionfish. It can hide some of its arms in the sand but leave two arms out. Then with its white and brown stripes and the two arms, it looks like a sea snake! It can also pull its arms together and swim on the sea floor, so to a predator, it looks like a poisonous flatfish!

Like other octopuses, the mimic octopus has eight arms and three hearts. It swims by shooting out jets of water through a siphon. It also has a large brain for its size. That's one smart octopus!

Weird but true

One kind of spider tricks predators by imitating an ant. It holds two legs up to look more like an ant when it walks.

A mimic octopus imitating a poisonous flatfish

leafy sea dragon

14 **Read and write.** Work with a partner. Compare your answers.

1. What does the leafy sea dragon imitate? ____________________
2. What does the leafy sea dragon use to swim? ____________________
3. What does the mimic octopus look like? ____________________
4. What does the mimic octopus do with its arms? ____________________

15 **Work with a partner.** Choose the leafy sea dragon or the mimic octopus to talk about. Your partner will listen and complete the first row. Then listen to your partner and fill in the second row.

Habitat	Shape	Color	Movement

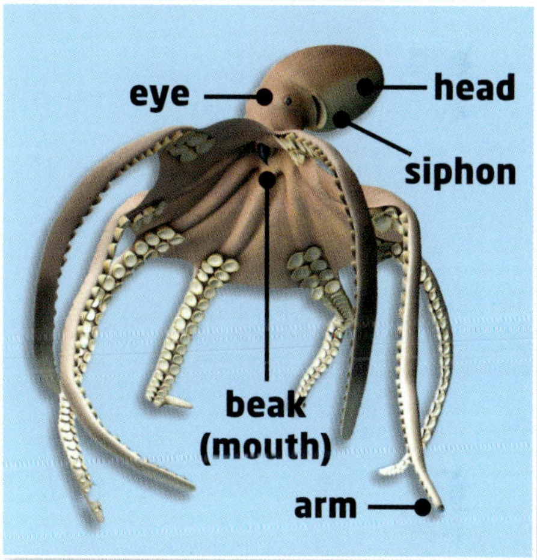

An octopus

16 **Work in groups of three.** Take turns. Summarize the reading.

Paragraphs of Classification

A paragraph of classification describes characteristics that members of a group share. You can define, compare, and contrast details to show how things belong to a group or class. You can use words such as *both, each of, like, but,* and *unlike.*

17 **Read.** Read about two types of copycat animals. How does the writer classify them? What words does the writer use to show their characteristics? Underline the words and expressions.

One or Two Ways to Imitate

Some animals copy other animals to avoid attack. They copy the things that predators avoid, such as a bad taste or a dangerous weapon. Some species copy the appearance of another animal, but not other characteristics. For example, the viceroy and the soldier butterfly resemble each other. They also both taste bad to predators. These types of animals imitate in two ways. The ash borer moth looks like a wasp, but it doesn't have a stinger. Predators avoid it, but it can't sting them. The ash borer moth belongs to the class of animals that only copies appearance.

viceroy butterfly

ash borer moth

18 **Write.** Write about animals that belong to a certain type. Describe the characteristics that they share.

19 **Work in a small group.** Share your writing.

NATIONAL GEOGRAPHIC

Mission

Protect biodiversity.

- Why is it important to preserve diverse species of animals?
- How does biodiversity affect your community?
- Work in a small group. Discuss a local species of animal. Think of ways to protect it. Discuss and write the best ideas in the box.

- Work with another group. Share your ideas. Are they the same or different? Which ideas does everyone like best?

"We need to increase people's interest and awareness about wildlife and conservation issues and reduce the general disconnect from nature."

Krithi Karanth
Conservation Biologist
Emerging Explorer

tarsier

20 Make a classroom mural.

1. Work in small groups. Choose a habitat such as an ocean, a forest, or a desert.
2. Discuss how animals protect themselves in that place.
3. In your part of the mural, show some animals that use camouflage and some that survive in other ways.

Now I can . . .

- ◯ describe animal features.
- ◯ describe how animals protect themselves.
- ◯ talk about ways animals imitate others.
- ◯ write a paragraph of classification.

Unit 3

Music in Our World

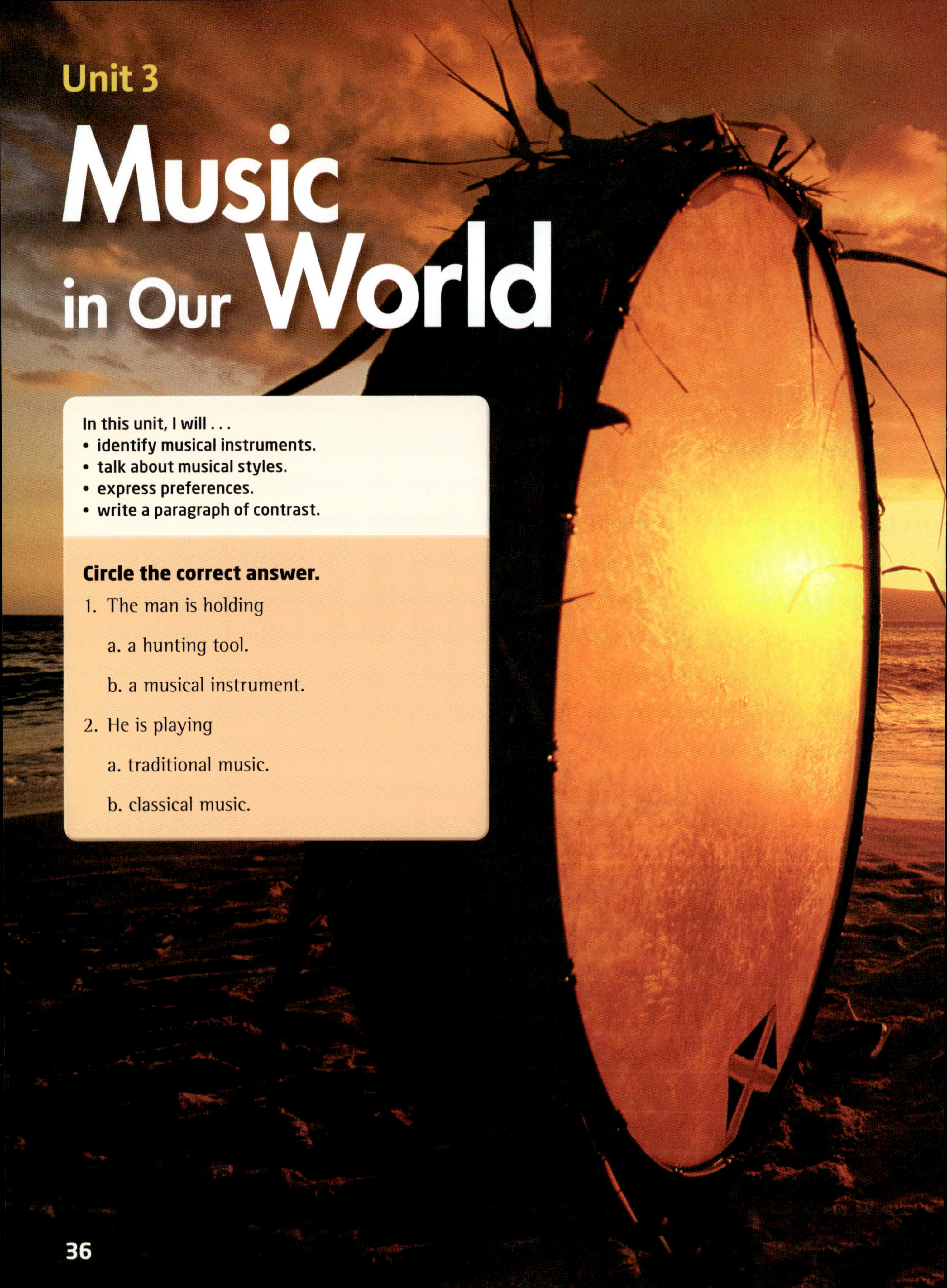

In this unit, I will . . .
- identify musical instruments.
- talk about musical styles.
- express preferences.
- write a paragraph of contrast.

Circle the correct answer.

1. The man is holding

    a. a hunting tool.

    b. a musical instrument.

2. He is playing

    a. traditional music.

    b. classical music.

Makena Beach, Maui

1 Listen and read. TR: A19

2 Listen and repeat. TR: A20

There are three main types of musical instruments. String instruments make music when you pluck the strings. Wind instruments make sounds when you blow air through them. Percussion instruments make different sounds when you hit them or shake them.

Music has its own language. Each single sound is a **note.** Play two notes or more at one time to make a **chord.** A string of notes and chords played one after the other makes a **melody.** The thump, thump, thump that makes you want to dance is the **beat.** Combine them all, slow and fast over time, and you have **rhythm.**

a guitar

a flute

a drum

Do you want your **band** to play better? You have to **practice!** Play songs again and again until they sound really good. When your band sounds good, you can **perform** for an audience. Invite your friends to the **concert!** If you don't play an instrument but you have a good voice, you could be the **lead singer!**

3 **Work with a partner.** What did you learn? Ask and answer.

4 Listen, read, and sing. TR: A21

Music Is Fun

Have you ever listened to hip-hop?
Have you ever listened to drums?
I listen to all kinds of music.
It's amazing fun.

Listen to the saxophone.
Listen to the beat.
Listen to the melody.
Feel it in your feet!

The flute is playing.
The piano is, too.
I can hear the guitar.
Can you?

CHORUS

Listen to the rhythm.
Listen to that band!
Sing the notes (la la la)
and clap your hands.

Have you ever played a note?
Have you ever played a chord?
Have you ever played a rhythm:
1, 2, 3, 4?

CHORUS

5 **Work with a partner.** Ask and answer.

1. Who are your favorite musicians?
2. What instruments do they play?
3. Why do you like their music?

Drummers, Ninga, Burundi

GRAMMAR TR: A22

Have you **ever listened** to hip-hop? — Yes, I **have.**
Have you **ever danced** to hip-hop? — No, I **haven't.**
Have you **ever been** to a concert? — No, I **never have.**
Has Lisa **ever heard** an orchestra perform? — No, she **has never heard** an orchestra perform.

6 **Read.** Complete the sentences.

1. This song is new. I have never heard (hear) it before.
2. I ______________ (go) to see an opera. I don't think I'd like it.
3. ______________ (listen) to jazz? Yes, I like it!
4. If you ______________ (hear) her sing, then you know she sings well.
5. This is his first time. He ______________ (perform) in public.
6. ______________ you ______________ (dance) to a slow song?

Chinese opera

7 **What about you?** Write questions. Work with a partner. Answer each other's questions.

1. go / rock concert ___Have you ever gone to a rock concert?___
2. play / a musical instrument ______
3. take / music lessons ______
4. watch / a band ______
5. listen to / classical music ______
6. sing / in public ______
7. hear / your brother sing ______
8. perform / in public ______

8 **Work in groups of three.** Use words from the list to ask and answer. Take turns.

band	guitar	dance	play
concert	piano	have jazz lessons	sing
drums	saxophone	listen to	take
famous	singer	meet	watch

9 **Listen and repeat.** Then read and write. **TR: A23**

hip-hop

classical

pop

jazz

rock

1. A large orchestra that includes cellos, violins, a piano, basses, and trumpets often plays ______________________ music.
2. Some music uses spoken words instead of singing. It's called ______________________.
3. A type of music with swing and rhythm that began 100 years ago and had links to the music of West Africa is ______________________.
4. This music is made for many, many people to enjoy. It's easy to listen to. It's ______________________ music.
5. We call this music with a strong beat and fast rhythm ______________________.

10 **Work with a partner.** Talk and stick. Rank the types of music (1 = most favorite). Discuss your favorite music and give examples of songs and performers.

1	2	3	4	5

GRAMMAR TR: A24

He sings **more loudly than** I do.
I play the guitar **as well as** my brother.
She plays the violin **better than** he does.
He practices piano **less often than** I do.

11 **Read and write.** Make comparisons. Use five words from the list.

beautifully   fast   hard   often   slow   well   worse

1. He's good. He plays guitar ____________________ he plays the drums.
2. That's not good. The orchestra sounds ____________________ the band.
3. She practices ____________________ than he does. She plays at least twice a day.
4. I dance hip-hop ____________________ I dance rock.
5. I play the piano ____________________ my older sister.

12 **Play a game.** Play with a partner. Take turns. Spin and make sentences with a comparison.

13 **Listen and read.** TR: A25

It's All Music

People made music before they could write about it. The oldest instrument ever found is more than 35,000 years old. It's a flute. Instruments of this type are called wind instruments. Like the sound of the wind, the music comes from moving air. Some wind instruments have a special piece for your mouth. The piece also helps to make the sound. Each instrument has a shape that makes its sound different. Some wind instruments have holes for fingers. Others have buttons to press. Holes and buttons let you change the way the air travels to change the melody.

Another way to make music is with strings. When you slide a finger over a string or pluck it, it makes music. Most string instruments have thick or thin strings and long or short strings to make different notes.

The shape of the body of a stringed instrument also helps to make the sound. Musicians use a bow to play some string instruments. The bow is a piece of wood with hairs or a string stretched between its ends.

You can also make music by hitting or shaking something that makes a sound. Percussion instruments can be made from many things. That's because most things make a sound when you hit them. An empty space inside the instrument makes the sound louder. Percussion instruments with strings make music when the strings are hit. A drum is a percussion instrument. A piano is a percussion instrument, too. When piano keys are pressed, hammers inside the piano hit the strings to make music.

Woman playing guzheng, Xi'an, China

14 Choose the best answer.

1. A drum is a __________.

   a. string instrument   b. percussion instrument   c. wind instrument

2. If you press a key on a wind instrument, the sound changes because __________.

   a. your finger is heavy

   b. it holds the instrument tightly

   c. the path for the air changes

3. An empty space inside percussion instruments makes the sound __________.

   a. softer   b. faster   c. louder

4. Some string instruments are played with a __________.

   a. bow   b. hammer   c. key

15 **Match the instruments and their types.** Work with a partner. Check the correct column.

	Wind	String	Percussion
Drums			
Flute			
Guitar			
Piano			
Saxophone			
Violin			

weird but true

Mozart composed his first song when he was four years old.

16 **Work in groups of three.** Invent a unique band that mixes different musical instruments. What six instruments would you choose?

Paragraphs of Contrast

Paragraphs of contrast show the differences between things. You can use facts and descriptive details to contrast different characteristics. You can also use words like *but, although, unlike, while, instead,* and *in contrast* to show things are not the same.

17 **Read.** Read the paragraphs about two ways to compose music. How does the writer show they are different? Underline the words used.

Composing, Then and Now

In the past, composers traditionally created their music with paper and pen. But now, technology — such as computer and phone apps — is changing how music is made. Although some composers still write by hand, more and more are using these new tools. Before, a composer would write notes on lined measures of music. In contrast, apps let the composer hum a melody, and then the apps write the musical notes!

Many people think that composing music was more difficult in the past. When composers wanted to make changes as they wrote, they had to stop and erase notes. It was a messy, slow process. Some new apps, unlike old erasers, make correction easy. These apps can show music as a moving stream of color. To make changes, the composer can pull and twist music with his or her fingers on the screen. While a traditional composer is busy cleaning ink off fingers, a modern composer can write more songs instead!

18 **Write.** Write about two styles of music or two musical instruments. How are they different? Use words and expressions that show contrast.

19 **Work in a small group.** Share your writing.

NATIONAL GEOGRAPHIC

Mission

Change through music.

- Work with a partner. How does music change how you think and feel? How can music make the world a better place?
- Choose a song that changed how you think. Write some words of the song in the box.

"Music can change the world. It can inspire people to care, to do something positive, to make a difference."

Jack Johnson

National Geographic Arts Ambassador for the Environment

- Discuss how and why the song changed you.

20 Make an instrument.

1. Work in small groups and research homemade musical instruments.
2. Collect trash and junk, and make a musical instrument.
3. Join other groups with instruments and practice.
4. Have a concert!

We made percussion and wind instruments. They sound awesome!

Now I can . . .

- ◯ identify musical instruments.
- ◯ talk about musical styles.
- ◯ express preferences.
- ◯ write a paragraph of contrast.

Review

1 **Carla is doing a survey about music.** What are her questions? What do Laura and Andres answer? Complete the chart. **TR: A26**

Questions	Laura	Andres
1.	hip-hop	
2.		
3.		He likes to sing. He sang in public once.
4.	none	

2 **Do a survey.** Ask two other students the same questions. Take notes.

3 **Work in groups of three.** One of you is going on vacation to a place with extreme weather. How are you going to prepare? Take turns to ask questions and give advice.

hurricane
sandstorm
flood
ice storm
heat wave
ever
blizzard
never
tornado
plan
tropical storm

I'm going to Antarctica! That's cool, isn't it? Have you ever been there?

No, I've never been there. What are you going to pack?

I'm going to bring very warm gloves!

If you go to Antarctica, you need more than warm gloves!

4 **Match the copycat animal.** Find the photo that matches the text.

1. This animal's skin is as rough as a tree. And it is brown like a tree, too! That helps it hide from predators.
2. This animal has feathers as brown as the color of wood. If it hears you, it doesn't move. It makes its body stiff. It looks just like a tree branch!
3. This animal imitates the color of a dead leaf. It uses the leaf as camouflage. Even if you look for it, you will never see it!

5 **Continue the story.** Work in groups of four. Choose a story. Read it aloud. Then, add your own sentence to the story. Take turns. Then share your story with another group.

It is raining hard. Paolo runs under a tree. Maria is already standing there, too. They can hear thunder. Then, there is a flash of lightning! Maria says ...

A few friends met to play music. Paolo is good at playing guitar. Maria has a pretty voice. Alba has a drum. They talk about what music to play.

Let's Talk

It's my turn.

I will . . .
- take turns.
- give commands.
- talk about who won a game.

1 **Listen and read.** TR: A27

Marco: **Whose turn is it?**
Amy: It's my turn.
Marco: Well, **hurry up!**

Amy: **Yay, I won!**
Marco: Now **we're tied.**
Amy: **No way.** What do you mean?
Marco: Well, I won last time!

Whose turn is it? It's my turn. It's his / her turn.	**Hurry up!** Come on!	**Yay!** **I won!** **We're tied.** Sorry, you lost!	**No way.** That's not true. That's not possible.

2 **Work with a partner.** Use the chart. Take turns to talk about playing a game.

Who's going to take notes?

I will . . .
- talk about a classroom task.
- make a request.
- offer to do something.

3 Listen and read. TR: A28

Sonia: So, I'll be the reporter. **Who's going to** take notes?

Olga: **I'll do that.**

Sonia: Thanks. **Can you** watch the time, Hans?

Hans: Sure.

Hans: Um, **what page are we on?**

Olga: **We're on page** 25. We're sharing ideas about music.

Hans: Thanks, Olga.

<table>
<tr><td rowspan="3">Who's going to
________ ?
Can you
________ ?</td><td rowspan="3">I'll do that.
I'll (watch the time).
I'll be ________ .
I can ________ .</td><td>What page are we on?
Which page is it?</td><td>We're on page
________ .</td></tr>
<tr><td>How long do we have?</td><td>We have ________ .</td></tr>
<tr><td>What are we doing?</td><td>We're ________ .</td></tr>
</table>

4 Listen to two discussions. Circle what the students are doing. TR: A29

1. They are **a.** doing a role play. **b.** doing a crossword. **c.** preparing a poster.
2. They are **a.** doing a role play. **b.** doing a crossword. **c.** preparing a poster.

5 Work in groups of three. Prepare and practice discussions.

Choose one task. Discuss how you are going to do it.

1. Make a musical instrument from recycled objects.
2. Make a mural about copycat animals.
3. Make a poster about the weather.

Unit 4

Life Out There

In this unit, I will . . .
- discuss life in space.
- discuss space exploration.
- express my opinion.
- write a persuasive paragraph.

Circle the correct letter.

1. What are they looking at?

   a. the clouds b. the stars

2. What time of the day is it?

   a. late afternoon b. the middle of the night

3. Why are they wearing coats?

   a. They are on the moon. b. It's cold.

The Milky Way

2 Listen and repeat. TR: A31

Earth is a **planet** that moves around the sun. Other planets also **orbit** the sun. The sun and planets make up our **solar system.** The sun is a star like the stars you see in the sky at night. Some stars have solar systems with planets, too. There may be another planet out there that has an **atmosphere** with oxygen to breathe.

A star and the planets that orbit around it make up a solar system. Stars and solar systems make up a **galaxy.** Our galaxy is the Milky Way. It has about 100 billion stars. Outside our galaxy, there are more galaxies! There are more galaxies in the **universe** than there are stars in a galaxy. How many? We don't know! There are too many, and many are too far away to see.

A **comet** is a cloud of rock, ice, and gas that orbits the sun. Many earth years pass in its **journey** around the sun. Scientists keep **data** on comets to know when they will appear.

Think of the many galaxies in the universe. Think of the many stars in each galaxy. Think of the many planets that orbit the stars. Do you think that **extraterrestrials** may live on one of the planets? Many people **debate** this question.

3 **Work with a partner.** What did you learn? Discuss.

4 **Listen, read, and sing.** TR: A32

Deep in Outer Space

Let's all take a journey
past the atmosphere,
beyond our solar system,
far away from here.

We might find a new planet.
We might find a new place.
We might find things we've never seen
deep in outer space.

Deep in outer space,
who knows what we might find?
Deep in outer space,
deep in outer space!

Somewhere in the universe
we might find a moon
where flowers grow.
You never know,
but I wish we'd get there soon!

CHORUS

But right here on planet Earth
life is all around.
Our world is full of color,
texture, light, and sound.

We can take a journey
right outside our door
and see the wonder of life on Earth
and so much more!

CHORUS

Deep in outer space.

5 **Work with a partner.** Talk about life in outer space. Take turns.

- moon
- planet
- solar system
- universe

Rosette Nebula

GRAMMAR TR: A33

If a planet has an atmosphere, it **may** have life.
There **might** be life on other planets.

Do you think astronauts **might** go to the moon again?
Yes, but it **may** be very simple life.

6 **Read.** Check the true sentences.

1. Some stars may have planets like Earth. ☐
2. We may find extraterrestrials on a distant planet. ☐
3. A meteor might hit Earth. ☐
4. The Milky Way might be a galaxy. ☐
5. Earth may have an atmosphere. ☐
6. You may become an astronaut. ☐

7 **Complete the sentences.**

are	is	live
may be	may discover	may live

1. There ______________ oxygen in planets in other galaxies.
2. There ______________ no oxygen on the moon.
3. Extraterrestrials ______________ on other planets.
4. Astronauts ______________ in the space station for some time.
5. There ______________ other solar systems in the universe.
6. One day, scientists ______________ life on other planets.

8 **What do you think?** Write sentences.

1. green skin/extraterrestrial Extraterrestrials might not have green skin like they do in the movies.

2. comet/lifetime ______

3. universe/galaxies ______

4. comet/our planet ______

5. find/life ______

9 **Work in groups of three.** Take turns. Make a sentence about life in the universe. Your partners will add more information.

10 **Listen and repeat.** Then read and write. **TR: A34**

a space station

SETI: **Search** for ExtraTerrestrial Intelligence

1. A powerful ________________________ is needed to send anything into space.
2. People live and work in the ________________________. They perform experiments in space.
3. Extraterrestrials probably would not speak English. It would be difficult to ________________________ with them.
4. I saw a documentary about the ________________________ for life in other galaxies.
5. Someday we may land a ________________________ on the moon again.
6. Anyone who travels through space is an ________________________.

11 **Listen and stick.** Work with a partner. Take turns describing the rocket liftoff. **TR: A35**

GRAMMAR TR: A36

Did **everyone** see that comet?
Someone will go to Mars one day.

Does **anyone** want to be an astronaut?
No one can see all the stars in the universe.

12 **Read and write.** Complete the paragraph.

anyone everyone no one someone

______________ likes to debate about life on other planets. ______________ knows for sure if there is life out there or not. If ______________ tells you that they know, that person really doesn't know! Are you ______________ who likes to debate? I will debate about life in space with ______________ who wants to. ______________ knows the answer, but ______________ has an opinion!

13 **Work with a partner.** What about you?

1. Does anyone in your family think there is life on other planets?
2. Name one thing everyone in your family does.
3. Name one thing no one in your family believes.
4. Name a funny habit someone in your family has.

14 **Play a game.** Cut out the cards on page 165. Make sentences. Take turns.

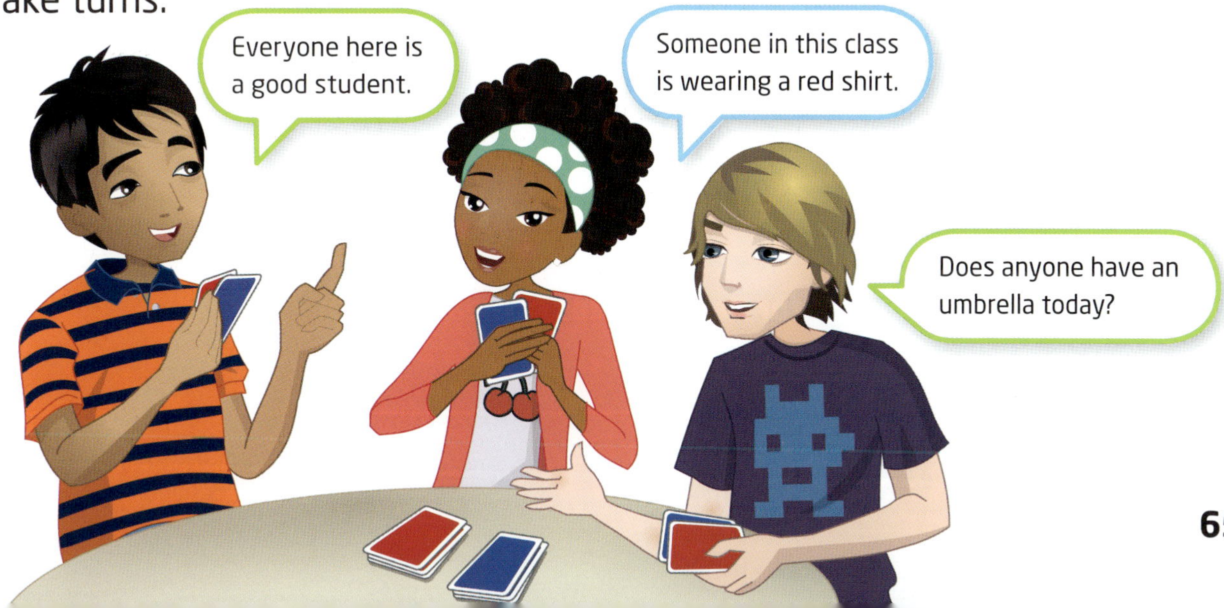

15 **Listen and read.** TR: A37

Listening for Life

If extraterrestrials live on other planets, we can't see them. Planets in other solar systems are extremely far away. We can't see the planets, even with our biggest telescopes. But what if the extraterrestrials want to communicate with us? What if they are sending messages? This signal would travel through space. After many years, it might reach our solar system. The signal would be very weak. It would be hidden in the noise from other places in space. We would need special tools to hear it.

Scientists at SETI have made a tool for listening. It uses 42 satellite dishes that are connected together. Scientists plan to have 350 dishes one day. They point all the dishes at the same place in the sky. Then they search for any data they can hear. The dishes can hear very weak signals. For example, they could hear a cell phone on a planet in our solar system. (That's if someone had a cell phone on Jupiter!) The dishes pick up noise from radios on Earth, too. Scientists must be careful to avoid this noise.

We have not heard from an extraterrestrial yet. But is it possible that they are listening to us? If they are, most could not have heard us yet. We have used radios for less than 100 years. That's not much time for the big distances in the universe. In that time, our signal could only reach a small number of stars. Extraterrestrials from nearby solar systems would not hear us for thousands of years.

Length of Time Needed for Radio Waves to Reach Earth

16 Check T for *True* and F for *False*.

1. Extraterrestrials have listened to our radio waves for over 100 years. (T) (F)
2. SETI dishes listen for life by listening for radio signals. (T) (F)
3. Scientists point the SETI dishes in many directions. (T) (F)
4. Radio waves from Earth are a problem for SETI scientists. (T) (F)

17 **Should we search for life?** Write why and why not.

I think it's a good idea to search for life because . . .	I think it's a bad idea to search for life because . . .

18 **Work with a partner.** Look at the chart and discuss. Support your opinion.

weird but true The first astronauts were fruit flies. They were launched on February 20, 1947.

Paragraphs of Persuasion

In persuasive paragraphs, you write to convince the reader of your opinion. To persuade the reader, you use facts to support your opinion. Write strong sentences that show you believe in what you are saying. Introduce your facts with expressions such as *research shows, according to,* and *the facts show that.*

19 **Read.** How does the writer persuade? Underline the words.

Forever Searching

Long ago, people thought that the sun and planets orbited Earth. We like to think that we are at the center of things. But scientists studied the stars carefully. Their research shows that we are not at the center. Copernicus was the first to say that Earth orbits the sun. He was right. And the sun orbits the center of the galaxy. The universe has many stars that we can't see. And, according to some NASA scientists, somewhere there may be life.

Why do we search? The facts show that we have always been people who search. For example, Zheng was an explorer from China who traveled as far as Arabia and the Horn of Africa in the 1400s. Frederick Cook went to the North Pole in 1908. And Roald Amundsen traveled to the South Pole in 1911. We search both on Earth and in space because we like to find answers. And a big question is, are we alone? We will search until we know.

20 **Write.** Do you think we should search for life in space? Take a position. Think about cost, usefulness, urgent problems on Earth, and so on. Use facts to persuade.

21 **Work in a small group.** Share your writing.

NATIONAL GEOGRAPHIC

Mission

Live curious.

- Think about things you want to know. How can you find answers?
- Work with a partner. Discuss. Do you search for answers even when it's difficult? How do you feel when you finally find the answer? Write your ideas in the box.

____

____

____

____

____

- Work with another group. Share your ideas. Are they the same or different? Which idea does everyone like best?

"We finally have the tools and technology to answer this age-old question: Are we alone? Jupiter's moon Europa is a beautiful place to go and explore that question."

Kevin Hand

Planetary Scientist/Astrobiologist

Emerging Explorer

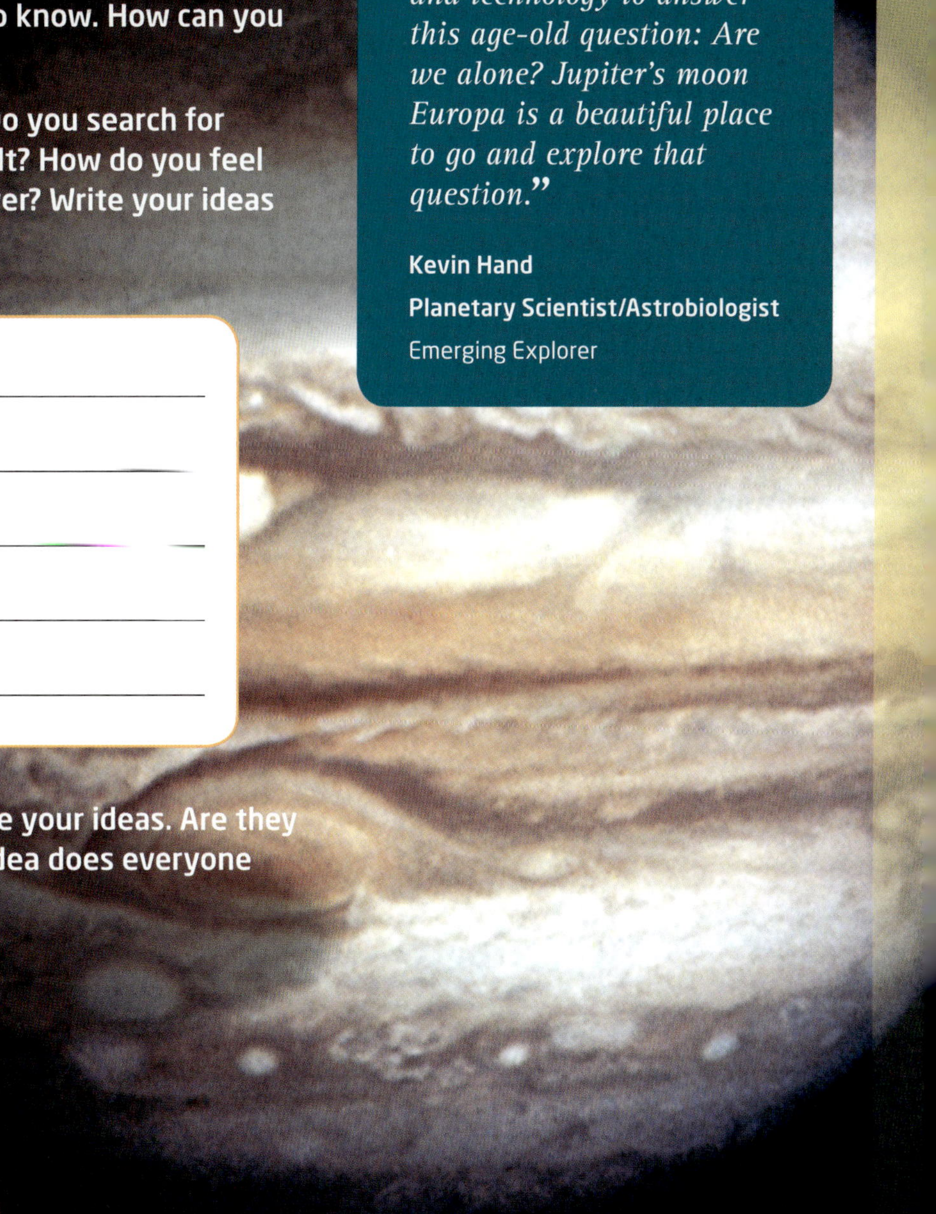

Jupiter

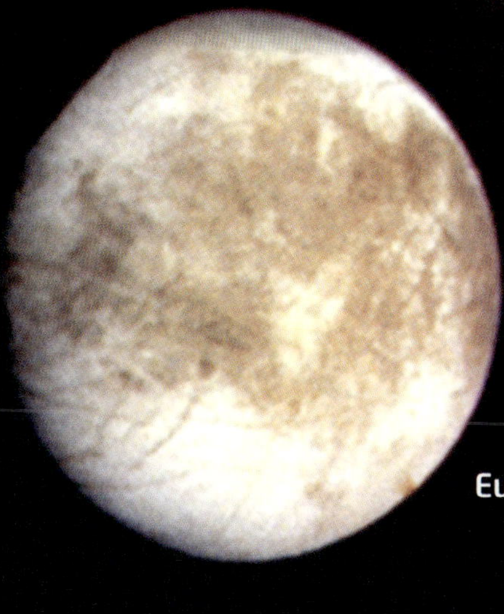

Europa

22 Research and make a model of a type of place where you think we could find life.

1. Choose a type of place you think might have life.
2. Research information.
3. Use the information you find and your imagination to re-create the surface of the type of planet or moon you choose. Use cardboard, paper, and other materials.
4. Draw different life forms as you imagine them.

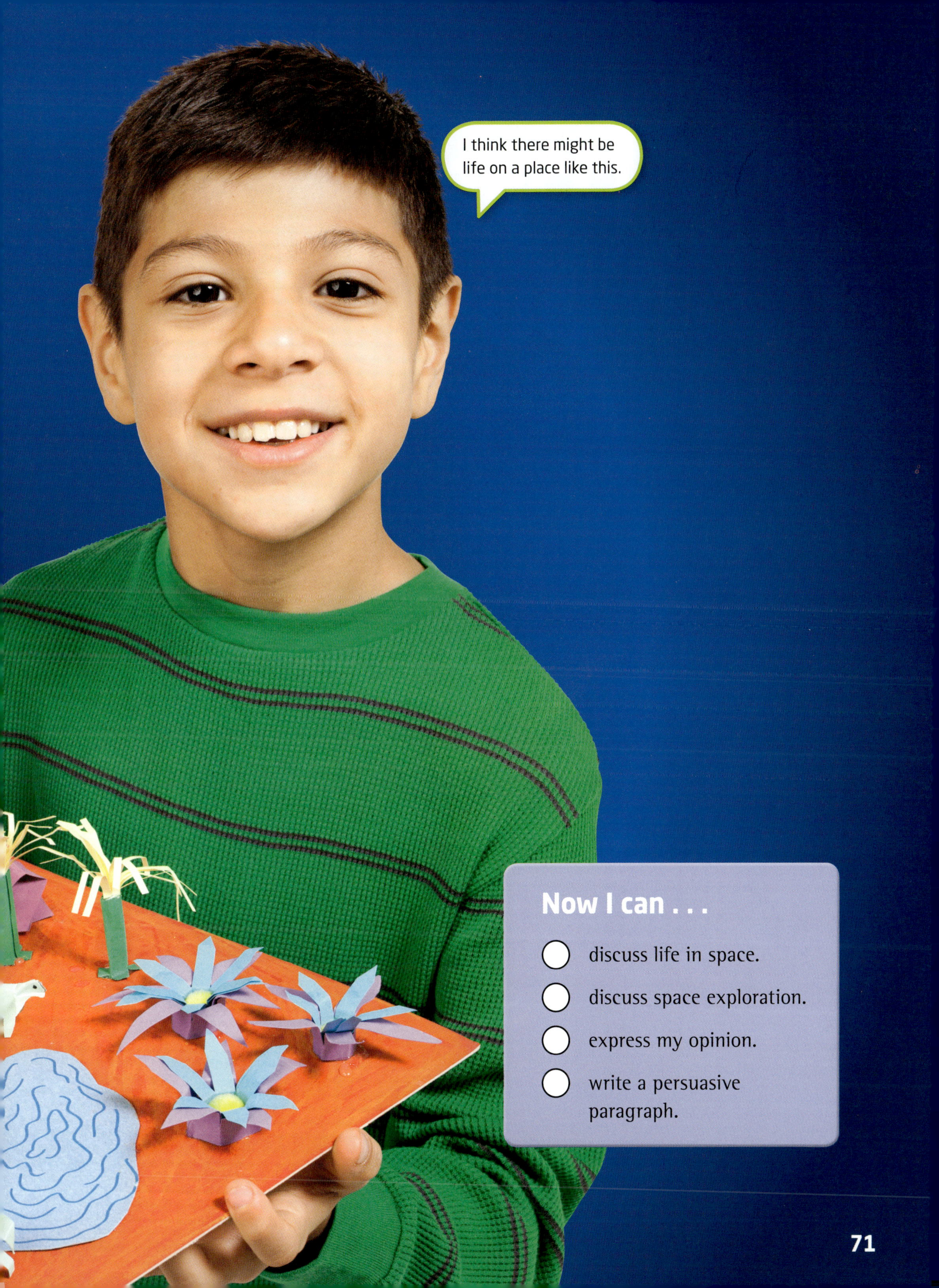

Now I can . . .

- ◯ discuss life in space.
- ◯ discuss space exploration.
- ◯ express my opinion.
- ◯ write a persuasive paragraph.

Unit 5

Arts Lost and Found

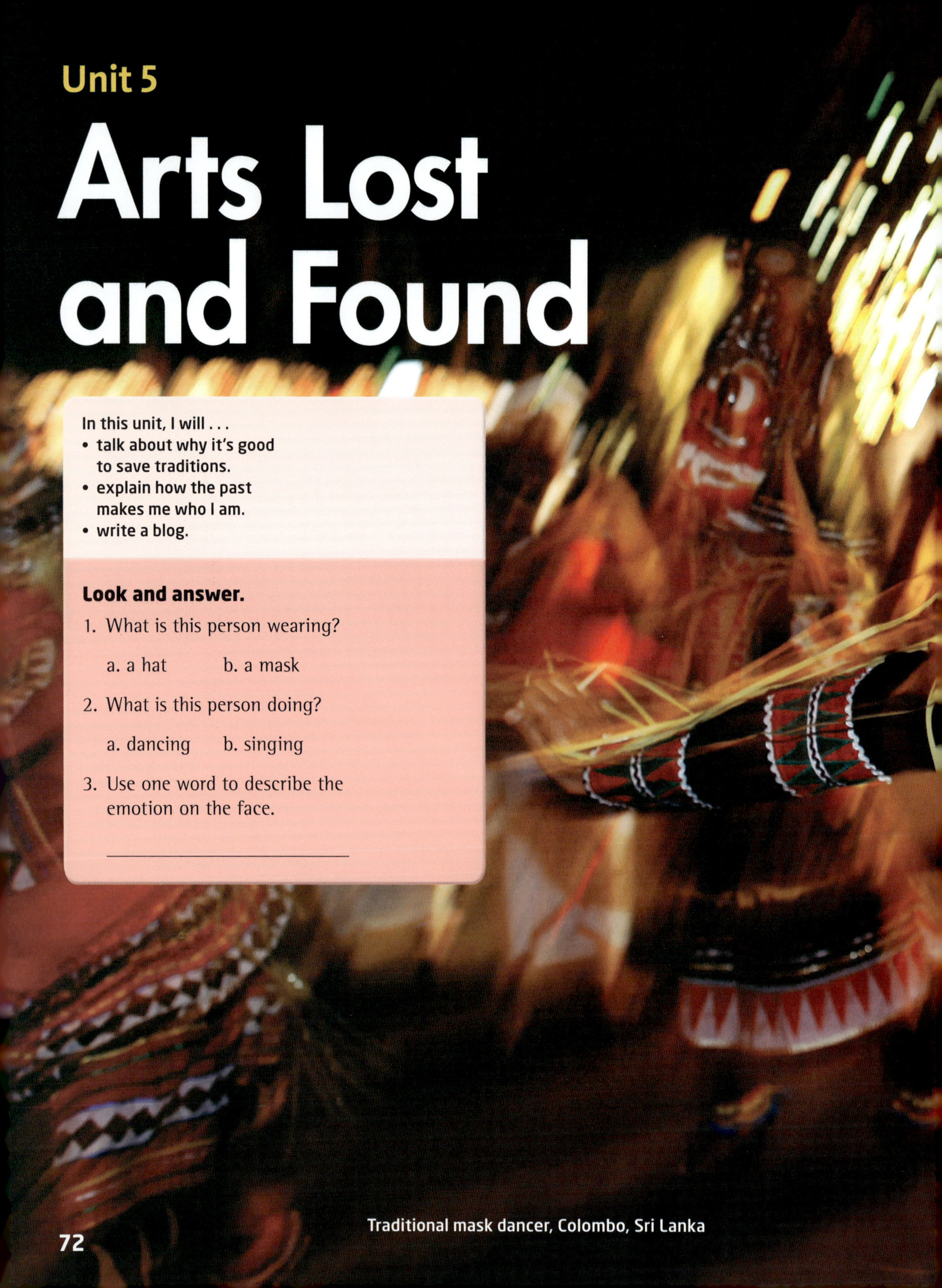

In this unit, I will . . .

- talk about why it's good to save traditions.
- explain how the past makes me who I am.
- write a blog.

Look and answer.

1. What is this person wearing?

   a. a hat b. a mask

2. What is this person doing?

   a. dancing b. singing

3. Use one word to describe the emotion on the face.

   ____

Traditional mask dancer, Colombo, Sri Lanka

1 Listen and read. TR: A38

2 Listen and repeat. TR: A39

Everyone should be **proud** of who they are. What makes you who you are? Part of who you are comes from the past. It comes from the **culture** of your parents, grandparents, and people before them. It comes from the **language** you speak, the **art** you see, the stories and music you hear, and the **traditions** you **share.**

Dragon boats are a 2000-year-old Chinese tradition. Racers must cooperate and row together to win. Today dragon boat racing has become a modern world sport.

Storytelling isn't always done with words. In Laos, dancers tell stories with their hands. The dances are part of their history. This history is **passed down** from one **generation** to the next.

The people of Tabasco, Mexico, keep their history alive. This **local** boy has clay on his face. He will do the jaguar dance to bring rain. His people speak an old language that came from the Olmec thousands of years ago.

The people of Ghana **hold on** to their tradition of **weaving** beautiful cloth. **Tourists** come to Ghana to buy cloth. The money that the tourists pay helps the **future** of the **community.**

3 Work with a partner. What did you learn? Discuss.

4 Listen, read, and sing. TR: A40

Keep Your Culture Strong

Knowing your history is important.
Holding on to your culture is an excellent thing!
Knowing your history is important.
It's up to you to keep your culture strong!

What special art does your culture bring to our world?
What special thing does your family bring to our world?
Weaving? Learn to do it!
Storytelling? Learn to tell it!
What brings your culture pride?

CHORUS

What special art does your culture bring to our world?
What special thing does your family bring to our world?
Embroidery? Learn to sew it!
Sculpture? Learn to sculpt it!
What brings your culture pride?

Your grandparents may seem old to you,
but they know a thing or two!

CHORUS

5 Work with a partner. Ask and answer.

1. What special art does your culture bring to our world?
2. What special thing does your family bring to our world?
3. What would you like to learn to do?

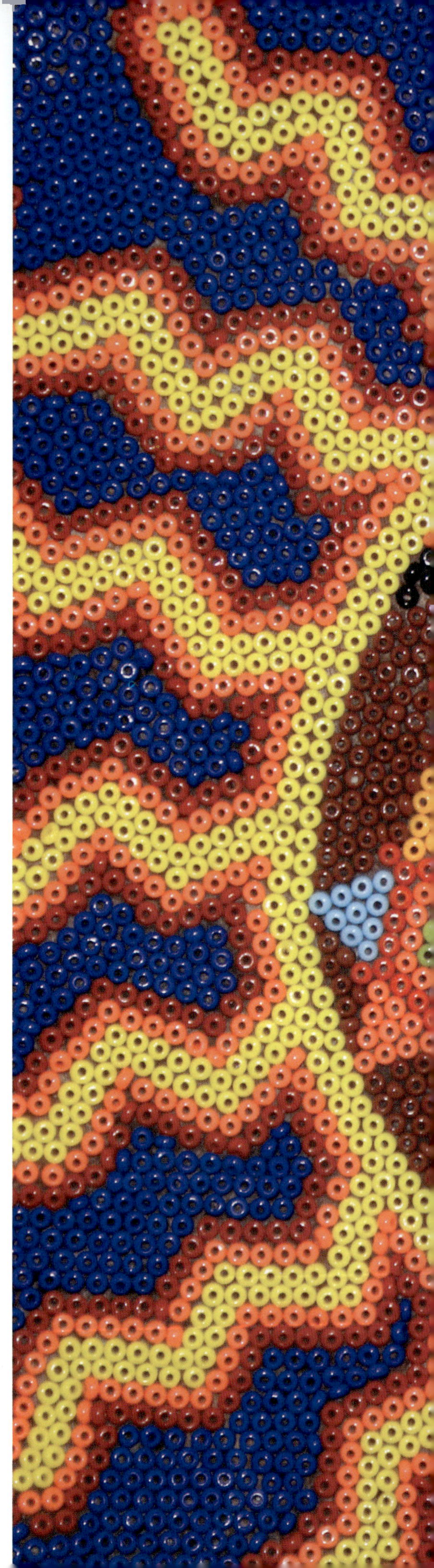

GRAMMAR TR: A41

Knowing your history is important.
Holding on to your traditions is a good thing.
Passing down family stories connects generations.
Creating art is a good way to share your culture.

6 **Read.** Complete the sentences.

cook make paint row share weave

1. ______________________ a boat is hard to do with another person.
2. ______________________ cloth was my grandmother's work.
3. ______________________ art is exciting!
4. ______________________ your traditions helps other people understand you.
5. ______________________ on wood is fun for people who like colors.
6. ______________________ traditional recipes is another way to keep your culture alive.

7 **What about you?** Complete the sentences about you and your family.

1. Painting is my father's hobby.
2. Teaching ______________________.
3. Cooking ______________________.
4. Helping ______________________.
5. Taking photos ______________________.
6. Reading ______________________.

8 Complete the conversation.

Mario: Grandpa, did you **listen to music** when you were a kid?

Grandpa: Yes, I did. ______________________ was one of my favorite hobbies!

Mario: And did you **go to the movies?**

Grandpa: Of course! I went every Sunday. ______________________ was the most important event of the weekend!

Mario: Did you **talk** to your friends **on the phone?**

Grandpa: No, I didn't. ______________________ was very expensive when I was a kid!

Mario: And did you **play sports?**

Grandpa: Not much. My parents thought that ______________________ was a waste of time. They wanted me to study all the time! But I still played soccer with my friends!

Mario: How about chores? Did you **help around the house?**

Grandpa: Of course! ______________________ was something everyone had to do!

9 **Work in groups of three.** Take turns. Express your opinion.

listening to stories	making art	saving traditions	visiting family
watching dancers	singing traditional songs	looking at old photos	

10 **Listen and repeat.**
Then read and write. **TR: A42**

handcrafted

sculpture

embroidery

pottery

jewelry making

1. When a work of art is made by hand, we say it's ____________________.
2. People use ____________________ to make their clothes more beautiful and decorative.
3. ____________________ is made from clay that dries and becomes hard. Sometimes it is heated in an oven.
4. To make a ____________________, artists can use materials such as wood, stone, metal, or ice.
5. ____________________ is popular. Most kids like to make bracelets.

11 **Look, rank (1 = most favorite), and stick.** Work with a partner. Discuss your preferences.

1	2	3	4	5

GRAMMAR TR: A43

My friends are good at **making** jewelry.
I like **eating** traditional foods.
My mother enjoys **embroidering** clothes.
I'm interested in **learning** about new places.

12 **Read and complete the sentences.** Use the words from the list.

cooperating making passing sharing storytelling traveling

1. Young people today are very interested in ______________ their traditions.
2. I'm very excited about ______________ to the country of my grandparents.
3. Do you like ______________? Storytellers like ______________ down their traditions.
4. I enjoy ______________ traditional jewelry.
5. We can save our rich history by ______________ with people from traditional communities.

13 **Play a game.** Cut out the cube on page 167. Work with a partner. Take turns making sentences.

14 Listen and read. TR: A44

Modern Music with Ancient Roots

Did you know that modern music comes from traditional music? Every generation changes the music of the past. They make it their own. Reggae music began in Jamaica, but it has its roots in African music. Africans came to Jamaica and brought their music. It mixed with music from Europe. Now, reggae impacts music all over the world. Dancehall and hip-hop music came from reggae!

Shaabi music is based on Egyptian folk music. It is played with the saxophone and electronic keyboard, which are modern instruments. But it is also played with a kanun, a traditional string instrument. The instruments are different, but the musical roots are the same!

Norteño is a modern type of Mexican music with folk roots. Old Norteño music was played with an accordion and a Mexican guitar. Then Norteño bands heard rock music. They added drums, saxophones, and electronic keyboards to their bands! Modern Norteño has a stronger beat than the traditional music.

In Japan, many people listen to J-pop music. J-pop is the name for all modern Japanese pop music. It includes many modern music types and instruments like electric guitars and keyboards. In the 1920s, when Japanese pop music began, performers used harmonicas and string instruments. The music combined Western jazz and soul with a traditional style of Japanese singing. Today every J-pop artist or band selects and combines the instruments and music rhythms they like best with their Japanese-language songs.

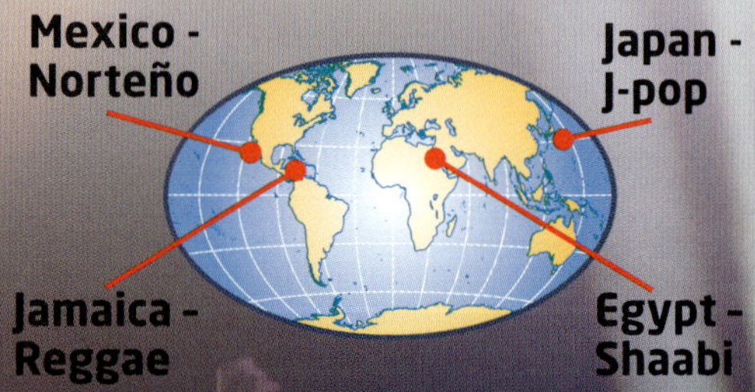

15 Read and write.

1. Where did reggae music begin? ______________________________
2. In what country is Norteño performed? ______________________________
3. What kind of music influenced J-pop? ______________________________
4. Which music is based on Egyptian folk music? ______________________________
5. Which music influenced dancehall and hip-hop? ______________________________

16 **Compare the music.** Work with a partner.

Mice sing to each other at night.

17 **Work with a partner.** Make new music. Invent a new musical style. It can be completely new, or you can modernize a style you know. What styles would you mix? What instruments would you use?

Blog Entries

In a personal blog, you write about your thoughts. You describe what you saw, heard, or felt. A blog sounds like an informal conversation. You can ask your readers to post a response on your blog. You can use expressions like *so cool, awesome, hated it,* and *laugh out loud (lol).*

18 **Read.** What informal expressions does the writer use in her blog? Underline them.

« » Cecilia's Blog

The coolest vacation ever!!!

My family and I went to Machu Picchu in Peru. It was awesome. First, I took a long train ride with my family to Aguas Calientes. From there we took a bus to Machu Picchu. The bus went slowly up the steep mountain. (I'm really glad the bus was slow.) LOL. From the bus window I saw llamas eating grass.

When we arrived, I was excited. It was so cool to see the ruins. The Incas who built Machu Picchu were great architects. My family and I climbed the stairs all the way up to the Sun Gate. It was a steep climb. We stopped to rest a few times because I was incredibly tired. At the top, it was wonderful. We could see everything! I think my photos are fabulous. Tell me what you think.

19 **Write.** Write a blog entry about a family vacation or a special day. Describe your thoughts and feelings.

20 **Work in a group.** Share your writing. Listen and take notes.

NATIONAL GEOGRAPHIC

Mission

Value your cultural traditions.

- Work with a partner. What local culture and traditions are in danger?
- Why should we keep our culture and traditions alive? List some ideas in the box.

- Work with another group. Share your ideas. Are they the same or different? Which ideas does everyone like best?

"I'm committed to protecting the cultures of the world in hopes that the wisdom of their elders is remembered."

Elizabeth Kapu'uwailani Lindsey
Filmmaker/Anthropologist
National Geographic Fellow

21 Make a time capsule of things that show your culture.

1. Work in small groups.
2. Talk about things that show your culture.
3. Choose the best things to include.
4. Put objects in your time capsule.

Now I can . . .

- ◯ talk about why it's good to save traditions.
- ◯ explain how the past makes me who I am.
- ◯ write a blog.

Unit 6

Amazing Plants!

In this unit, I will . . .

- talk about how plants adapt.
- discuss the importance of plants.
- compare plants.
- write a descriptive paragraph.

Check T for *True* and F for *False*.

1. These flowers are sculptures. (T) (F)
2. The flowers are wet. (T) (F)
3. These flowers eat insects. (T) (F)

Australian sundew

1 **Listen and read.** TR: B2

2 **Listen and repeat.** TR: B3

Have you ever heard of a flower that smells like rotting meat to **attract** insects? Have you seen a plant close its **leaves** over an insect? Can plants really do these things? Let's learn more about the **behavior** of plants.

Plants need **light,** air, water, and nutrients to live. **Roots** absorb the nutrients that are in the **ground** and water. Tiny creatures called **bacteria** turn these nutrients into food that the plant can use. But some places don't have a lot of these nutrients. So some plants **adapt.** They follow a different plan for **survival.** Their **strategy** is to eat insects to live!

The stink lily gets its name from its smell. The flower **stinks** like rotting meat. The smell attracts flies to the plant—and then **tricks** them! When a fly crawls on the flower, pollen sticks to the fly. Then the fly takes the pollen and leaves it on the next plant it visits. That's how the stink lily makes new plants.

The Venus flytrap attracts insects with a sweet odor. When an insect lands on an open leaf, the leaf closes and **traps** the insect. Then the plant slowly **digests** the insect over a period of eight to ten days.

3 **Work with a partner.** What did you learn? Ask and answer.

4 Listen, read, and sing. TR: B4

Plants Are All Around

Leaf and stem and flower and root!
The sweet, delicious smell of fruit
is here and there and everywhere!
Plants are all around.

Plants are growing
up and down.
Air is flowing
all around.

Plants come in every shape and size.
Their bright colors attract the eyes
of bees and butterflies.

Big and small,
plants survive it all.

CHORUS

Some plants play tricks with our eyes.
They're made to give us a surprise.
A plant is designed to survive.
To make new seeds, to grow and thrive.

Some of the oldest plants on Earth
are trees on mountains high,
drinking in the light,
reaching up into the sky.

Leaf and stem and flower and root!
The sweet, delicious smell of fruit
is here and there and everywhere!
Plants are all around.

5 **Work with a partner.** Ask and answer.

1. Which plants do you like best?
2. Do you eat them?
3. What makes them special to you?

Passionflower

GRAMMAR TR: B5

Insects **are attracted** to the plant's sweet smell.
The seeds **are carried** away by birds.

How **is** the insect **trapped?**
The fly **is caught** inside the closing leaf.

6 Read and complete the sentences.

1. Plant food (make) ______is made______ by bacteria.
2. Pollen (take) ____________________ to other plants by insects.
3. The seeds (carry) ____________________ by birds.
4. Plants that eat insects (find) ____________________ in the rain forest.
5. Many new plants (discover) ____________________ every year.

7 Read and underline the answer.

Socotra **is located / is called** in the Indian Ocean. Many strange trees **are found / are needed** here. One famous tree **is attracted / is called** the dragon blood tree. It **is used / is found** to make paint and medicine. The desert rose **is used / is found** in the desert in Socotra. It has beautiful pink flowers. It **is shaped / is found** like the foot of an elephant!

Dragon blood trees

8 **Read and write.** Rewrite the sentences.

1. Plants need nutrients for survival.

Nutrients are needed by plants for survival.

2. Birds eat the fruit.

3. The plant attracts insects.

4. The smell of the stink lily tricks the flies.

5. The pitcher plant traps and digests small animals.

9 **Work with a partner.** How many sentences can you make? Take turns.

snacks	need	children
flowers	find	plants
insects	eat	flowers

10 **Listen and repeat.** Then read and write. TR: B6

a daisy

a vine

1. An outer part of a flower is called a ______________.
2. A climbing ______________ holds onto things as it grows.
3. Be careful! That ______________ is sharp.
4. The class gave the teacher a red ______________.
5. Is that flower a white ______________?

11 **Work with a partner.** Give a clue. Listen and stick. Take turns.

That's a pretty yellow flower!

It's a daisy!

1	2	3	4	5

GRAMMAR TR: B7

I don't want a plant **that** smells like rotting meat!
I like plants **that** trick and trap insects.

12 Read and write.

sunflower/stem   daisy/petals   garden/flowers   rain forest/vines
rose/thorns   tree/leaves   Venus flytrap/insects

1. A sunflower is a plant that has a long stem.
2. ______________________________
3. ______________________________
4. ______________________________
5. ______________________________
6. ______________________________
7. ______________________________

13 **Play a game. Work in groups of three.** Choose a page in this book. Describe an object. The group guesses what it is. The winner picks another page.

14 **Listen and read.** TR: B8

Is That a *Plant?*

The *Hydnora africana* has no leaves or stem. It has a flower that looks like a hungry mouth! Inside is white stuff that stinks. Insects are attracted to the smell. The insect is trapped inside the flower by stiff hairs. The insect eats the white stuff to survive. Pollen sticks to the insect. A few days later, the flower opens and the insect is free. Then it takes the pollen to another flower. The flower has done its job!

The white baneberry is also called "doll's eyes." Its fruit looks like eyes on blood red stems! It is round and white and has a black dot. Birds eat the fruit and spread the seeds. That's how the doll's eyes makes other plants. The fruit does not hurt the birds, but it's poisonous to people! If people touch any part of the plant, they will get blisters! Eating the fruit can stop a person's heart.

The *Rafflesia arnoldii* also has no leaves or stem. But it has the largest flower of all plants! It can grow to be 1 meter (3 feet) across and can weigh 11 kilos (24 pounds). The flower looks scary. Things that look like big thorns grow out of its center. And worse, it stinks like rotting meat—just like the stink lily! But this plant doesn't eat insects. The odor attracts insects that carry its pollen to other plants. This big flower blooms for only five days. Because there are fewer and fewer of these plants, they may become extinct.

White baneberry, North America

	Hydnora Africana	*Rafflesia Arnoldii*	White baneberry
Leaves and stems	no	no	yes
Poisonous	no	no	yes
Stinky	yes	yes	no
Flower size	6 cm (2.36 in.)	1 m (3.28 ft.)	10 cm (3.93 in.)
Fruit	yes	yes	yes

15 Check T for *True* and F for *False*.

1. The white baneberry has a stinky smell that attracts insects. Ⓣ Ⓕ
2. The fruit of the *Hydnora africana* is very poisonous. Ⓣ Ⓕ
3. The *Rafflesia arnoldii* has no leaves or stems. Ⓣ Ⓕ
4. Birds avoid the white baneberry. Ⓣ Ⓕ
5. The *Rafflesia arnoldii* eats insects that walk on it. Ⓣ Ⓕ
6. When the *Hydnora africana* traps an insect, it lets it go in a few days. Ⓣ Ⓕ

16 **Work with a partner.** Rank the coolest plants (1 = most favorite). Explain why.

Rank	Plant	Why the plant is cool
	Hydnora africana	
	Rafflesia arnoldii	
	Rose	
	Venus flytrap	
	White baneberry	
	Your choice ________	

17 **Invent a cool plant. Draw it and tell what it does.** Work in a small group. Share your plant.

weird but true: The *Welwitschia mirabilis* can live without rain for years. Some have lived for 2,000 years!

Descriptive Paragraphs

A descriptive paragraph tells what you see, feel, taste, and hear. You can organize your description of a person, place, or thing in different ways. You can describe the big parts first and then the small parts. You can go from big to small, from top to bottom, from the inside to the outside, and so on.

18 **Read.** Read about the sensitive plant. How does the writer describe it? How does the writer organize the description?

The Sensitive Plant

Did you know that some plants can move? The sensitive plant moves when you touch it. The stem has tiny white hairs, and it stands straight up. It grows to about 50 centimeters. It has many thin green leaves. Each thin leaf is made of many tiny parts. The parts are like tiny leaves. These tiny leaves grow on both sides of each leaf stem.

When you touch a leaf, the tiny leaves fold. Two by two, starting from where you touch, they close down. The leaf stem hangs down, too. It looks like it is hiding and doesn't want you to touch it. After a half-hour the plant stands up—until you touch it again!

Sensitive plant

19 **Write.** Write about the plant you invented. Describe it. Organize your description. Is your plant amazing? Why or why not? Explain.

20 **Work in a group.** Share your writing. Listen and take notes.

NATIONAL GEOGRAPHIC

Mission

Value plants.

- What plants are important in your community?
- Why are these plants important? How are they used?
- Work in a small group. Choose a plant. Discuss why it is important. Write your ideas in the box.

- Get together with another group. Share your ideas. Are they the same or different? Which idea does everyone like best?

"On my first trip to the rain forest I met a woman who was in terrible pain because no one in her village could remember which plant would cure her. I saw that knowledge was truly being lost, and in that moment I knew this was what I wanted to do with my life."

Maria Fadiman, Ethnobotanist

Emerging Explorer

Green tea

21 Make a local plant guide.

1. Work with a partner. Choose a local plant.
2. Research the plant. Collect or draw pictures.
3. Glue and label the pictures.
4. Describe the plant and how it is used.

Now I can . . .

- ◯ talk about how plants adapt.
- ◯ discuss the importance of plants.
- ◯ compare plants.
- ◯ write a descriptive paragraph.

Review

1 **Read.** Complete the paragraphs. Use words from the list.

adapt	embroidery	handcrafted	no one	tourists
anyone	extraterrestrial	hold on	strategy	trap
astronaut	galaxy	leaves	survival	weave

1. Do you think ______________ is listening to us from outer space? ______________ knows the answer to this question, but scientists are discussing the possibility of intelligent ______________ life.

2. The Huichol people in Mexico make traditional art to help them ______________ to their culture. Selling their ______________ art to ______________ helps the future of their community.

3. The resurrection fern has learned to ______________ to dry climates. When there isn't enough rain, it looks dead. But this is just a ______________ for ______________. The plant is alive! When it rains, the dry ______________ turn green.

2 **Work with a partner.** Practice and perform a role-play.

Student A:
You think there may be life on other planets.

Student B:
You don't believe there is life on other planets.

anyone	everyone	journey	no one	someone	universe
communicate	galaxy	may/might	planet	spacecraft	

I think there may be life on planets in other solar systems.

If you are right, why doesn't anyone from other planets communicate with us?

3 **Work with a partner.** Listen to true sentences. Then read the sentences below. Check T for *True* and F for *False*. **TR: B9**

1. Traditions are passed down from one generation to the next. Ⓣ Ⓕ
2. Languages must be protected from dying. Ⓣ Ⓕ
3. Some plants are trapped by flies. Ⓣ Ⓕ
4. Insect-eating plants are called carnivorous. Ⓣ Ⓕ
5. The possibility of human life has been debated by extraterrestrials for a long time. Ⓣ Ⓕ

4 **Work in small groups.**

1. Write eight definitions using the word *that* on strips of paper.
2. Cut the strips just before the word *that*.
3. Mix up the paper strips, and exchange your paper strips with another group.
4. Match the strips of paper, and read the sentences aloud. The group with the most correct sentences wins.

A rose is a plant | that has thorns.

An astronaut is a person | that travels to space.

5 **Write.** Choose four objects from the list. Write clues for your partner to guess.

comet	rocket	space station
jewelry	satellite	TV
pottery	sculpture	vine

This is something that many women wear on their ears or around their neck.

Jewelry!

Let's Talk

Can I borrow your bike?

I will . . .
- make an informal request.
- make an excuse.
- show understanding / accept "no" for an answer.

1 Listen and read. TR: B10

Lucia: Hey, **can I borrow** your bike this weekend, Roberto?

Roberto: Um, **I'm really sorry,** but it's new. My dad won't let me lend it.

Lucia: **That's OK. I understand.**

Lucia: Marcelo, **can you lend me** *your* bike?

Marcelo: **Sure. Go ahead.** But give it back on Sunday, OK?

Can I borrow . . . ? **Can you lend me . . . ?** Is it OK if I use . . . ?	**I'm really sorry.** I'm sorry, but . . . I can't. It isn't mine.	**That's OK. I understand.** No problem. Don't worry.
	Sure. Go ahead. Sure. Here you are! Yeah, you can borrow ________ . Sure. I can lend you ________ . Of course.	Give it back later, OK? Don't forget to give it back.

2 Work with a partner. Use the chart. Take turns to lend and borrow objects.

It could work.

I will . . .
- make a suggestion.
- agree and disagree.
- counter.

3 Listen and read. TR: B11

Lin: **I think we should** interview a scientist for our project.

Cheng: **That's a great idea.**

Mei: **Yeah, but** we don't have the time.

Jiang: **Actually, that could work.** My uncle is a scientist! I'll text him!

I think we should ______ .	**That's a great idea.**	**Yeah, but ______ .**	**Actually, that could work.**
I know what we should do! We should . . . Why don't we . . . ? What if we . . . ?	Why not? That could be good.	I don't think that'll work. I'm not so sure.	That might work. In fact, I think ______ . We could also ______ .

4 **Listen.** You will hear two discussions. Does everyone agree at the end of the discussion? Circle the answer. TR: B12

1. Yes No
2. Yes No

5 **Work in a group.** Prepare and practice discussions. Choose one of the three situations given below.

1. Let's interview a famous person!
2. Why don't we do a report with a big map?
3. I think we should paint a mural of volcanoes on the classroom wall.

Unit 7

Volcanoes

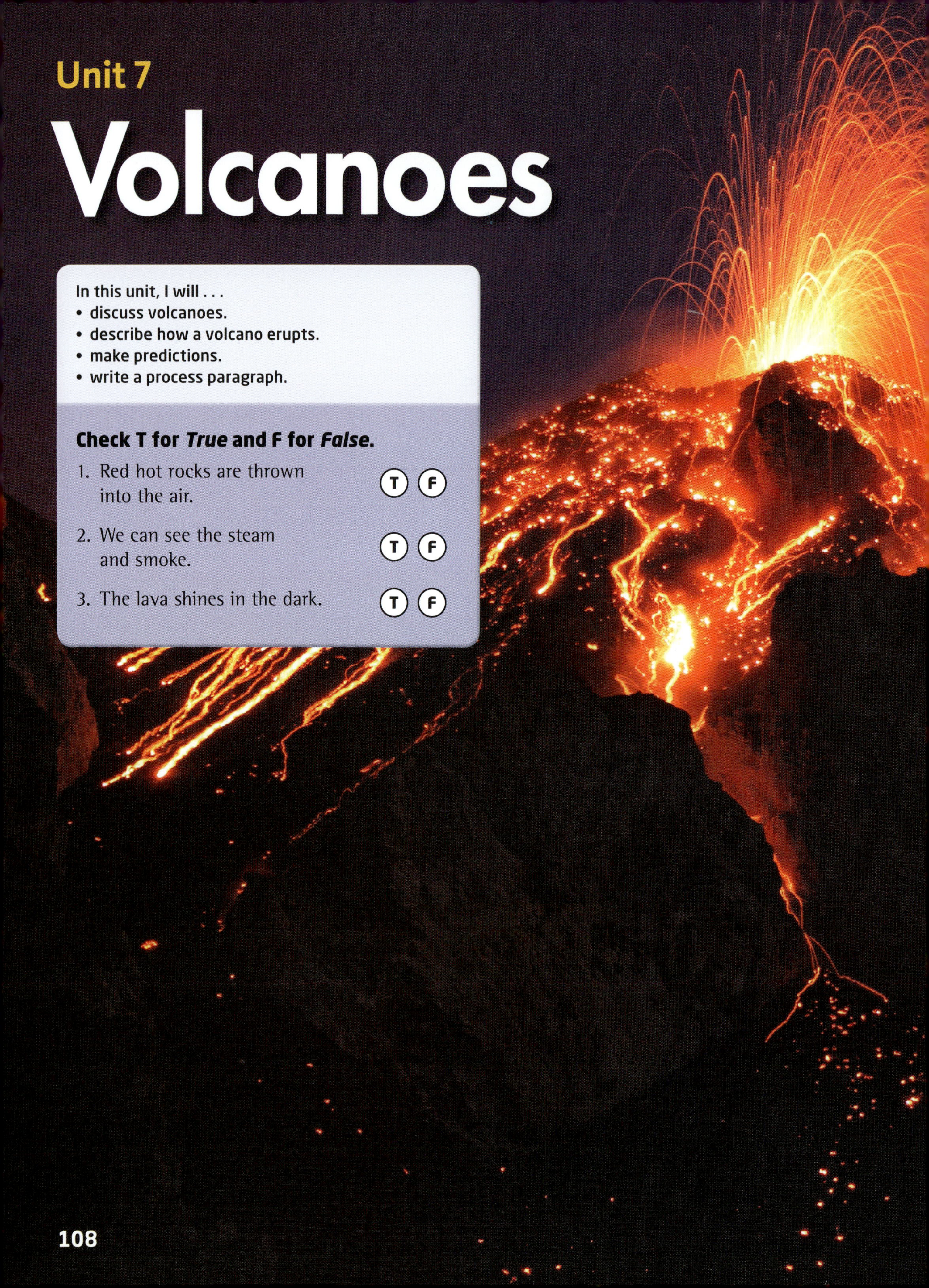

In this unit, I will . . .

- discuss volcanoes.
- describe how a volcano erupts.
- make predictions.
- write a process paragraph.

Check T for *True* and F for *False*.

1. Red hot rocks are thrown into the air. Ⓣ Ⓕ
2. We can see the steam and smoke. Ⓣ Ⓕ
3. The lava shines in the dark. Ⓣ Ⓕ

Stromboli volcano, Sicily, Italy

1 Listen and read. TR: B13

2 Listen and repeat. TR: B14

Go for a walk on a sunny day. The earth seems **calm** under your feet. But **deep** down, it is not. Under the earth's crust, it is so hot that rock is **melted.** This melted rock is called magma.

In some places there are deep **cracks** in the **surface** of the earth. These cracks let magma come to the surface. The magma pushes up the earth's crust. It **creates** a living mountain, a **volcano!**

A volcano **erupts** when magma **explodes** onto the surface. The flow of melted rock is called lava. The lava is thrown into the air and oozes down the volcano. The **heat** of the lava burns everything it touches.

The blast of an eruption throws **steam** into the air. The steam is created from water **inside** the earth. The blast also sends **gases** high into the sky. They make breathing difficult. A volcanic eruption can fill the sky with **ash**. Big eruptions **cover** the land **thick** with ash.

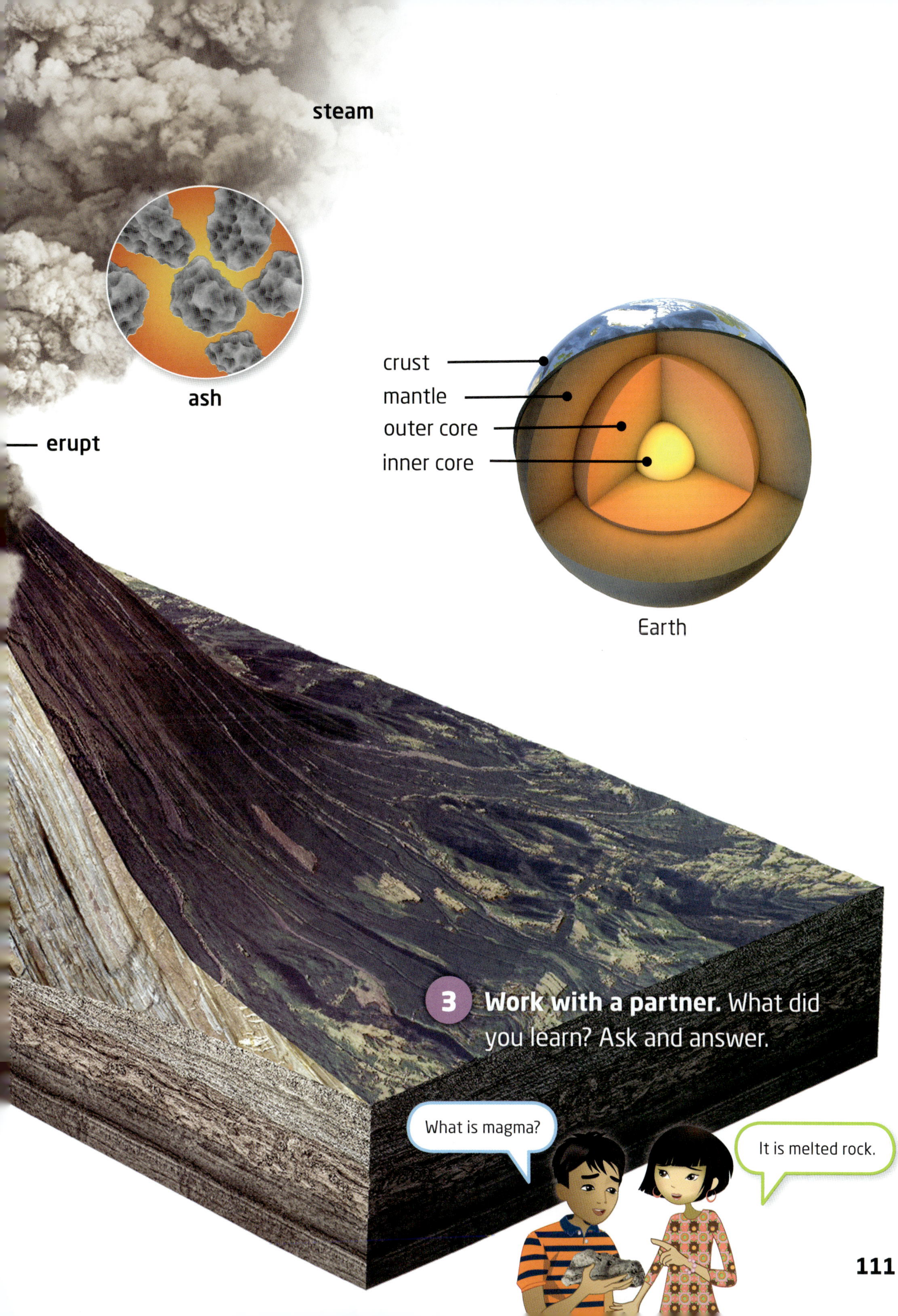

3 **Work with a partner.** What did you learn? Ask and answer.

4 Listen, read, and sing. TR: B15

Volcanoes Are a Lot Like Me

Volcanoes are a lot like me.
Some are awake and full of energy.
Other volcanoes are sleeping.
Yes, volcanoes are a lot like me!

When I get really silly,
and my energy builds up,
if it has no place to go,
sometimes I think I will explode!

Deep inside a volcano,
heat and gas are building up.
If they have no place to go,
the volcano will erupt!

CHORUS

If a volcano is dormant,
it's really just asleep.
A dormant volcano will sleep for centuries.

If a volcano is active,
it's very wide awake.
When it's awake, it's just like me.
It's ready to blow off some energy!

CHORUS

5 Work with a partner. Discuss.

1. Sometimes I'm like an active volcano because . . .
2. Sometimes I'm like a dormant volcano because . . .

Mount St. Helens, Washington, USA

GRAMMAR TR: B16

If the lava **touches** the trees, it **will** burn them.
If rain **hits** the lava, it'**ll** turn to steam.
I **will go** to a safe place **if** the volcano **erupts.**
The plants **will burn if** hot ash **covers** them.

6 **Read.** Write sentences.

1. I go to Hawaii / I see volcanoes

____

2. I run away / volcano erupts

____

3. ash covers the grass / the grass dies

____

4. lava reaches the sea / it makes steam

____

5. no airplanes fly / ash fills the sky

____

Kilauea, Hawaii, USA

7 **Write four sentence halves beginning with if.** Work in pairs. Take turns. Complete each other's sentences.

8 **Work in small groups.** Build each new sentence on the sentence before.

9 **Listen and repeat.** Then read and write. TR: B17

dormant

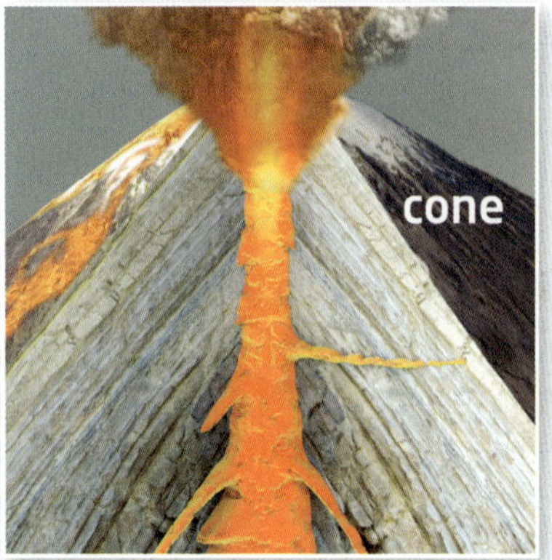

active

extinct

1. If a volcano is erupting, then it is ________________.
2. If a volcano is not erupting, but may erupt in the future, it is ________________.
3. If a volcano has not erupted in thousands of years and will not erupt in the future, it is ________________.
4. The hole left at the top of a volcano that has erupted is called a ________________.
5. The sides of a volcano form the ________________ at the top.

10 **Listen and stick.** Work with a partner. Discuss. TR: B18

How do you know a volcano is extinct?

You have to read about it before climbing!

1	2	3	4	5

GRAMMAR TR: B19

Because of the ash, the animals could not breathe.
The trees died **because of** the heat from the lava.

11 Read and write.

1. rocks flew into the sky / the eruption

____

2. the heat / no one could get close to the crater

____

3. it was difficult to see / the ash

____

4. we saw white clouds in the sky / the steam

____

5. the blast / the eruption could be heard from far away

____

12 **Play a game.** Play with a partner. Cut out the cards on page 169 and put them face down in a pile. Choose a card and start a sentence. Take turns. Complete your partner's sentences.

13 **Listen and read.** TR: B20

Active Volcanoes

There are active volcanoes all over the world. Some erupt often, sending hot lava down their slopes. People often live near these volcanoes. Because of the ash, the land is good for farming.

The longest erupting volcano is Mount Etna, in Sicily. It has been active for 3,500 years. Mount Etna erupts very often. It has destroyed many towns. People have tried to change the lava flow. They've built earth walls and used explosives. Some towns have avoided destruction. Successful evacuation plans have kept people safe.

Five volcanoes created the island of Hawaii. Mauna Loa is the largest volcano in the world. Kīlauea is one of the most active. In fact, it almost never stops erupting. The fumes from this great volcano are also a problem for local people.

The volcano Nyamuragira, in Africa, erupts about every two years. It also has big lava flows. It creates smaller volcanoes on its sides. At one time, the volcano had a crater with a lake of lava. Then in 1938, there was an eruption that opened up one side of the volcano. Because of the eruption, the lava lake flowed out of the crater. People do not live near this volcano.

Popocatepetl is about 70 kilometers from Mexico City. An eruption in 2000 made 50,000 people leave their homes. In 2012, Popocatepetl covered cars and streets with ash. Every March, people honor the volcano, offering it food and music.

weird but true **The largest known volcano is on Mars. It is about 22,000 m tall and 700 km across!**

Mauna Ulu, Hawaii, USA

14 Read and circle the letter.

1. This volcano had a lake of lava.

   a. Mount Etna   b. Nyamuragira   c. Stromboli

2. This is the largest volcano in the Hawaiian Islands.

   a. Mauna Loa   b. Kīlauea   c. Popocatepetl

3. This volcano's eruption caused the evacuation of 50,000 people.

   a. Nyamuragira   b. Popocatepetl   c. Puyehue

4. This volcano is the longest erupting volcano.

   a. Kīlauea   b. Vesuvius   c. Mount Etna

15 **Where are these volcanoes?** Work with a partner.

Kīlauea

Mount Etna

Nyamuragira

Mauna Loa

Popocatepetl

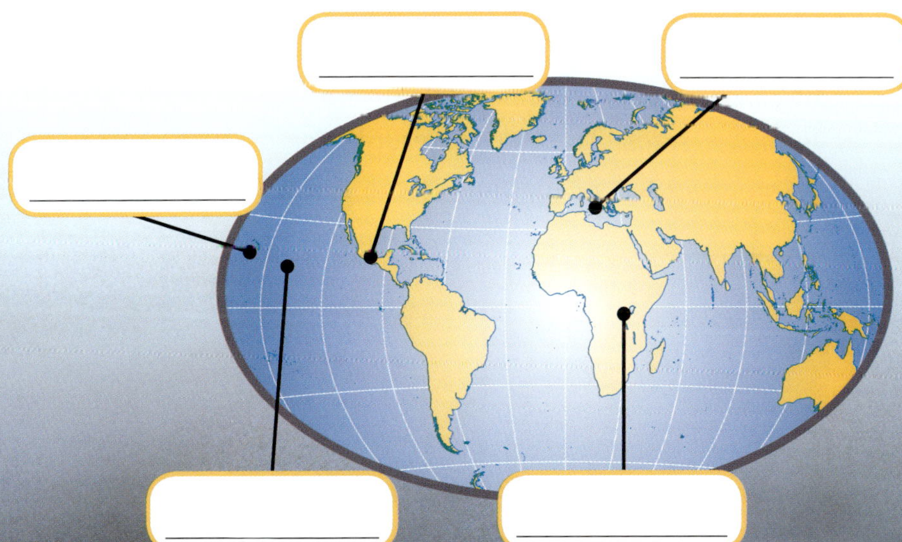

16 **Work with a partner.** Read the text again. Talk about two volcanoes. Take turns. Take notes.

Name of Volcano	Notes
1	
2	

Process Paragraphs

A process paragraph explains what happens in a sequence. It follows a series of actions from beginning to end. Use words such as *first, then, next, after, when, while, at the same time, now, before, as long as,* and *finally.* These words show the order in which actions or stages occur.

17 **Read.** Read the paragraphs about the stages of a volcanic eruption. How does the writer show the sequence of events? Underline the words.

How Volcanoes Explode

First, the heat deep inside the earth melts the rocks. Next, the trapped magma pushes on the top and along the walls of the volcano. At the same time, trapped gases push on the cone. There is no place for escape. When the pushing gets very strong, the walls get weak. After some time, the top of the volcano blasts away.

Finally, the magma and gases explode out the top. Gases and steam come out. The volcano throws ash high into the air. Lava flows down the sides. The volcano erupts for as long as the magma pushes. If there is a lot of magma, it can erupt for a long time.

18 **Write.** Describe a process that you know. Explain the steps from beginning to end.

19 **Work in a small group.** Share your writing.

NATIONAL GEOGRAPHIC

Mission

Help in a disaster.

- We hear about disasters all over the world. Work in a group. What can you do to help in a disaster?
- How can you get the community involved? Who can donate money or supplies? How could you send them to the disaster area? Write your ideas in the box.

"Crisis mapping can pinpoint urgent needs instantly, saving time and lives."

Patrick Meier, Crisis Mapper

Emerging Explorer

- Work with another group. Share your ideas. Are they the same or different? Which idea does everyone like best?

Mount Snowdon, Wales, UK

20 Make a model of an erupting volcano.

1. Get a cardboard tube about 4 cm wide and 20 cm long.
2. Cover the bottom of the tube with clay. Stick the tube up on cardboard.
3. Crush balls of newspaper. Tape them to the tube to make a cone.
4. Cover the cone with aluminum foil. Paint or glue sand on it.
5. Fill half the tube with baking soda.
6. Add red food color to vinegar. Pour it in the tube and watch it erupt!

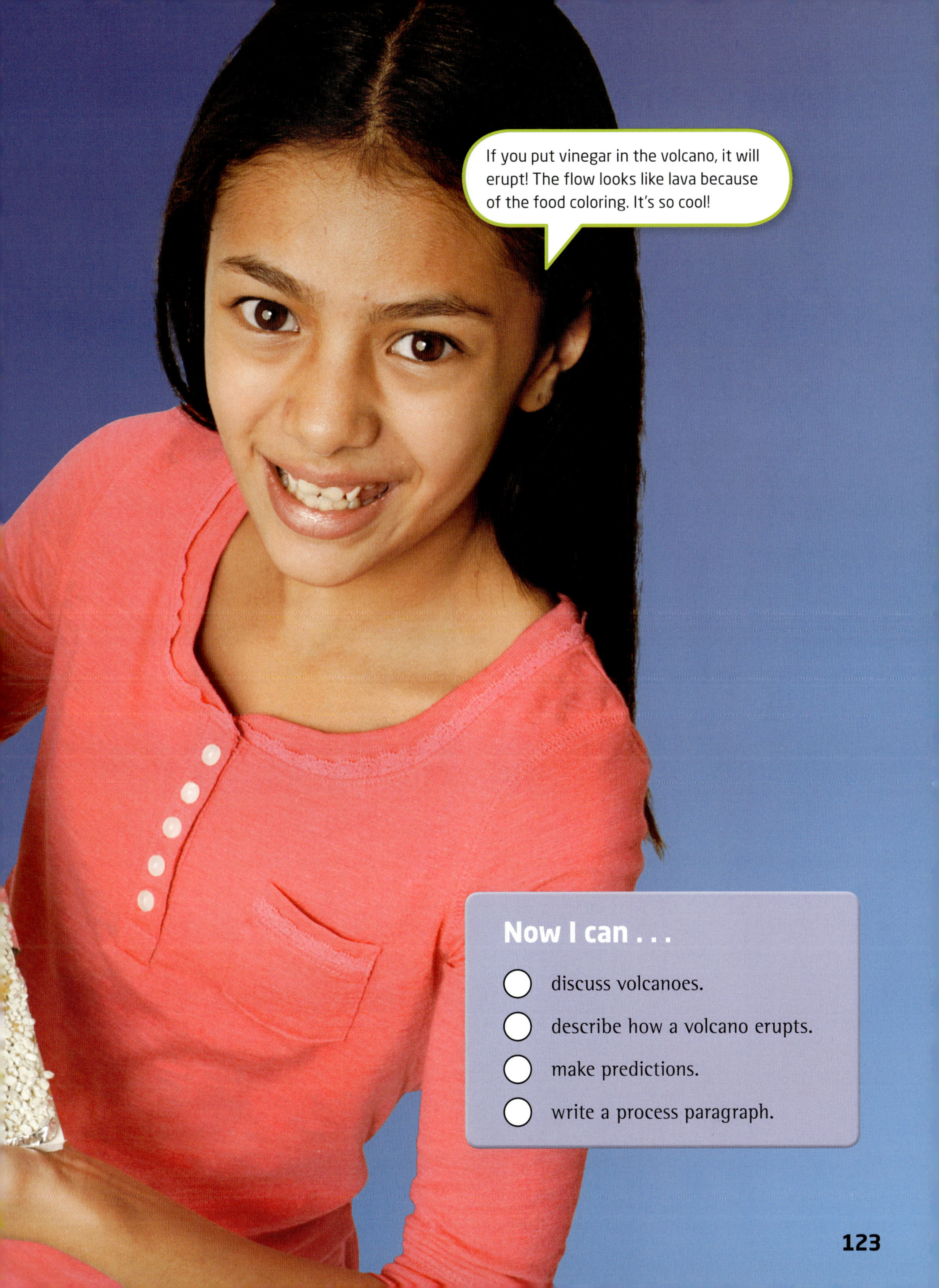

Now I can . . .

- ◯ discuss volcanoes.
- ◯ describe how a volcano erupts.
- ◯ make predictions.
- ◯ write a process paragraph.

Unit 8

Reduce, Reuse, Recycle

In this unit, I will . . .
- discuss the importance of reducing, reusing, and recycling.
- discuss art from recycled materials.
- talk about what I can do to help the environment.
- write a biographical paragraph.

Check T for *True* and F for *False*.

1. There are about one hundred sculptures. (T) (F)
2. Each sculpture is a little different. (T) (F)
3. The sculptures are made from trash. (T) (F)
4. This is a landfill. (T) (F)

HA Schult's *Trash People*,
Barcelona, Spain

1 Listen and read. TR: B21

2 Listen and repeat. TR: B22

Every day we make **trash.** Where does it go? Some of it is buried in **landfills.** Yuck! There has to be a better way! There is! You can choose a way of life that works with the **environment.** You can **conserve** instead of **throw away.** You can make **energy-efficient** choices!

The three Rs of the environment are ***reduce, reuse,*** and ***recycle.*** We all know about recycling. **Man-made** things are crushed and melted down. They are then made into new things. The best Rs are to reduce and reuse. Reduce by choosing to use less energy. Reuse by finding new uses for **junk.**

Choosing **natural** materials is friendly to the environment. Things made from natural stuff are cool! When they are used up, just like other trash, they go into the landfill, too. But they break down faster. And, natural things can be grown again. They're **renewable!**

Can we **design** things to reduce, reuse, and recycle? Yes! We can **build** houses that are energy efficient. We can make art with natural things, or reused things. The possibilities are endless!

3 **Work with a partner.** What did you learn? Ask and answer.

4 Listen, read, and sing. TR: B23

The Three Rs

When you're walking to the trash can
with some old stuff in your hand,
you might want to stop and think again.
Can this be reused or given away?
Let's start taking care of our world today!

Reduce. Reuse. Recycle.
Do it every day.
Don't throw everything into the trash
when clearly there's another way.

Reduce. Reuse. Recycle.
Help keep our world clean.
Do your part every day
to make our world green!

Recycling is easy when you know what to do.
Glass? Paper? Metal?
These things can be reused,
again, and again, and again!

CHORUS

Compost your uneaten food.
Composting isn't hard to do.
Natural things can be reused
when they get a helping hand from you!

Reduce. Reuse. Recycle.
Do it every day.
Don't throw everything into the trash
when clearly there's another way.

Reduce. Reuse. Recycle.
Help keep our world clean.
Reduce. Reuse. Recycle.
Help make our world green!

5 Work with a partner. Ask and answer.

How do you recycle, reuse, or reduce?

- glass
- paper
- metal

GRAMMAR TR: B24

Natural things **can be grown** again.
Many things **can be made** into art!

Aluminum cans **must be melted** to be recycled.
Some plastics **may be put** in recycling containers.

6 **Read.** Complete the sentences. Use the words in the list.

reused   made   colored   thrown away   built   conserved   designed

1. Clothes (can/color) ___can be colored___ with natural dyes.
2. Save the bricks that (can/reuse) ______________, and the broken ones (can/throw away) ______________.
3. Energy (may/conserve) ______________ by making good choices.
4. Fleece sweaters (can/make) ______________ from recycled water bottles.
5. Future cars (must/design) ______________ to run on electricity.
6. A house (can/build) ______________ with recycled materials.

7 **What things can be done to reduce, reuse, and recycle?** Use the words in the list. Write sentences.

"green" shopping bags	fix
magazine	reuse
water	recycle
energy-efficient houses	conserve
a faucet with a leak	design

1. Water can be conserved.
2. ______
3. ______
4. ______
5. ______

8 **Work with a partner.** Read one of your sentences. Your partner makes a sentence using the same verb. Take turns.

9 Listen and repeat.

Then read and write. TR: B25

chemicals

cardboard

metal

glass

tools

1. It is clear or colored. It can be melted down and reused. It is used to make bottles or windows. ____________________

2. It is made from paper. It is used to make shoe boxes. It is soft when wet.

____

3. They are used to clean things. They can hurt your skin. Don't drink them!

____

4. There are many kinds, and they have different uses. They help us do things that we can't do with just our hands. ____________________

5. This is used to make cans and also cars. It's used to make things that must be strong. ____________________

10 Listen and stick. TR: B26

1	2	3	4	5

GRAMMAR TR: B27

When we recycle trash, we save on materials and energy.
An artist's work may surprise us **when we first see it.**

11 **Read and write.** How do you and your friends help the environment? Use the words in the box.

bike	light	paper	plastic bottle	shopping bag	trash	water

1. When we leave the house, we turn off lights.
2. ______ when ______.
3. When ______, ______.
4. When ______, ______.
5. ______ when ______.

12 **Play a game.** Cut out the spinner on page 171. Work in a small group. Make sentences. Take turns.

13 Listen and read. TR: B28

Found Art

We often think of reusing and recycling as something we just have to do. But some people see it as a chance to create. Any object can be reused to make something amazing. Reusing is more than a way to save—it can help us think about things in new and different ways.

Using found stuff to make art is not new. *Found art* became popular in the 1900s. Found art made people think about the things around them in a different way. Many things could be made into art!

Today, many artists still make art from things they find. Sometimes they use things as they find them, and other times they make changes to the things they find. Sometimes they use junk. The artists put it all together to express their thoughts. We can enjoy their creativity and be amazed at the artists' skill. We can also be surprised by our feelings. Often we can just appreciate the beauty or the humor. All these things make found art valuable in our lives.

Recycling old aluminum cans into new ones uses 95% less energy than making new cans.

Artist Yong Ho Ji makes sculptures from rubber tires. He chooses real and imagined creatures to create.

14 Check T for *True* and F for *False*.

1. Using junk to make art is a way to reuse trash. (T) (F)
2. Found art always uses trash. (T) (F)
3. Art made from junk is valuable because it makes us think in new ways. (T) (F)
4. Found art started in the 1850s. (T) (F)
5. Brian Marshall makes sculptures from rubber tires. (T) (F)

15 **Label.** Use these words.

fork
key
pencil sharpener
spoon

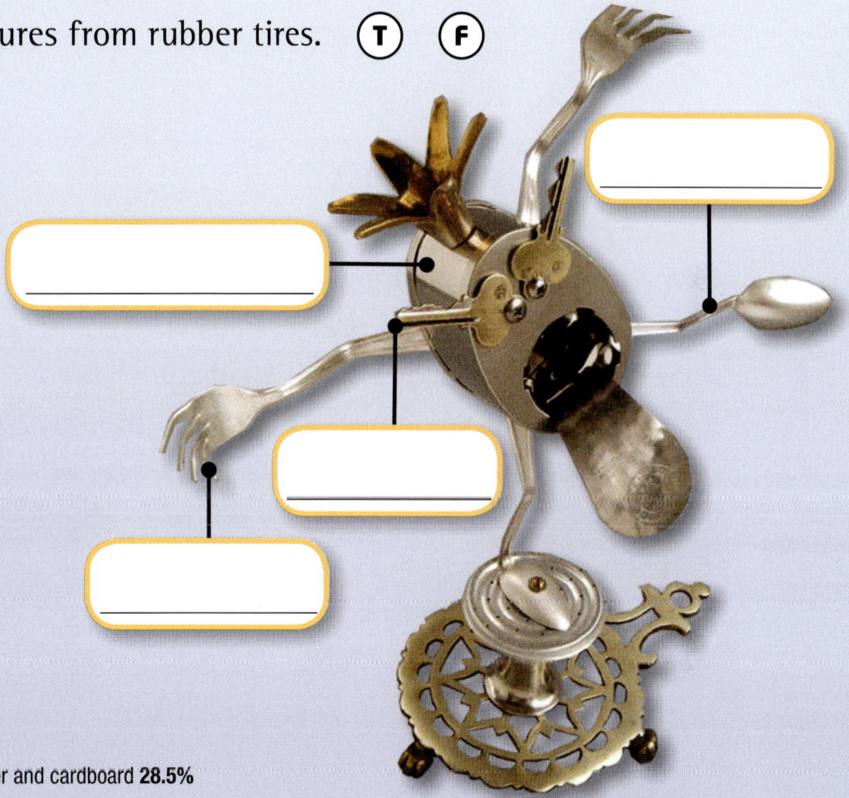

Artist Brian Marshall makes robot sculptures from found objects.

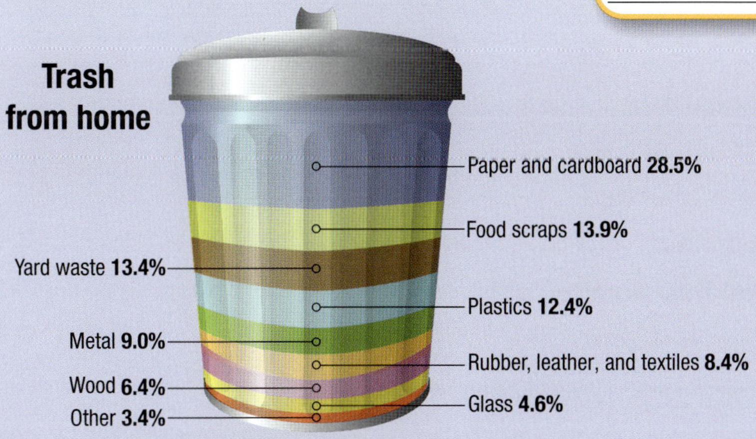

16 **Vote on the most creative work of art.** Work in a group. Look at these photos and the photo on pages 124 and 125. Discuss the art. Which do you like best? Explain why. Does your group agree?

17 **Make more trash art.** Work with a partner. Discuss creating trash art. What would you make, and what materials would you use?

Biographical Paragraphs

A biographical paragraph tells about the life and work of a person. You can include key dates, such as birth date, important events, and interesting facts in the person's life. You should also explain why this person is or was important. Use expressions such as *one of the most, famous,* and *the first.*

18 **Read.** Read about Marcel Duchamp. Find facts about his life. Identify reasons why he was considered important.

Marcel Duchamp

Marcel Duchamp was born in France in 1887. He was one of the most important modern artists of the 1900s. His first famous works were abstract paintings. These paintings showed a general idea of something, not objects the way people usually see them. This was a new way of making art, and many people did not understand it. It was shocking to many people.

Duchamp was the first modern artist to make art from things he found. He called these objects "readymades." His first readymade was the "Bicycle Wheel." At first, other artists said this work was not art. Duchamp shocked people! Later on, artists understood what Duchamp was creating. A version of this work of art is at the Museum of Modern Art in New York City.

Bicycle Wheel **by Marcel Duchamp, 1913**

19 **Write.** Write about an important or interesting person. Include important details and dates about the person's life. Explain why he or she is important.

20 **Work in a small group.** Share your writing.

NATIONAL GEOGRAPHIC

Mission

Help reduce our human footprint.

- What can your community do to reduce, reuse, and recycle?
- Think of ways your community can reduce waste. Think of ways it can reuse and recycle.
- Work in a group. Discuss ideas for the community. Write your ideas in the box.

"People have created the problem, so it's critical to get the public excited and eager to participate in a solution."

Alexandra Cousteau
Water Advocate and Environmental Filmmaker
Emerging Explorer

- Share your ideas with another group. Are they the same or different? Decide which ideas everyone likes best.

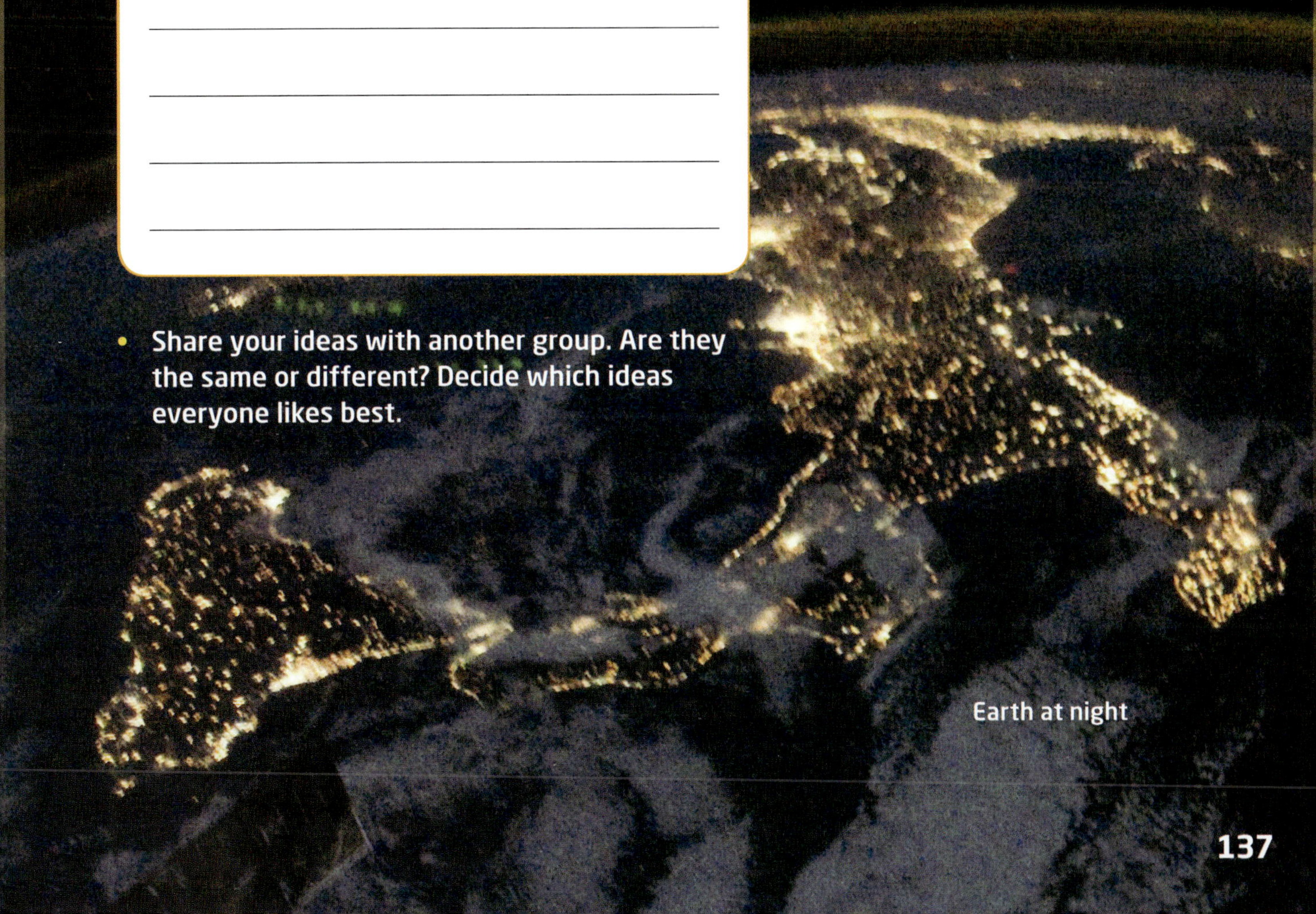

Earth at night

21 Make art from things you throw away.

1. Work in a small group. Collect different types of junk.
2. Look at your collected junk, and decide what to make.
3. Make your work of art.

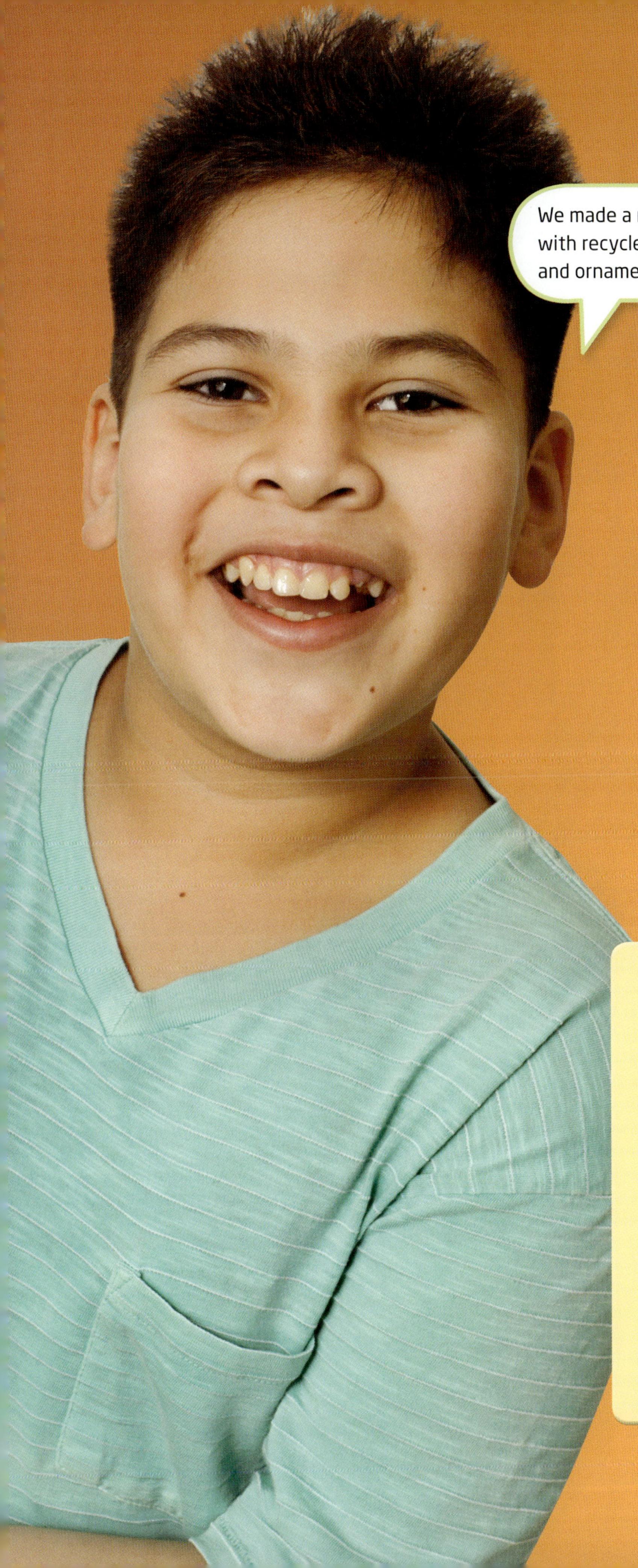

Now I can . . .

- ◯ discuss the importance of reducing, reusing, and recycling.
- ◯ discuss art from recycled materials.
- ◯ talk about what I can do to help the environment.
- ◯ write a biographical paragraph.

Unit 9

Cool Vacations!

In this unit, I will . . .

- talk about different vacation places.
- talk about what I would do in different situations.
- express preferences.
- write a review.

Look and circle the correct letter.

1. What are the people doing?
   a. playing in a pool
   b. sliding down a water slide
2. Where are they?
   a. at a water park
   b. at a river

Water park, Beijing, China

1 **Listen and read.** TR: B29

2 **Listen and repeat.** TR: B30

Do you like vacations with lots of people and noise? Or places that are quiet with no people nearby? Let's find out about some cool vacations!

The whole family enjoys **camping** together. Bring a **tent** and sleep outside. If you **hike** a very big mountain, you have to take a **guide** to help find the way.

Do you like history? Go see the **ruins** of an old city. If you like the modern world, take a **tour** of a city! But if you like to learn how to protect the natural world, then an ecotour is for you!

Do you like animals and plants? Go on a **photo safari** and take pictures of **wildlife**. Stay safe in a truck when there are dangerous wild animals.

A resort is a good place to **relax** and have fun on your vacation. Stay the night at a big **hotel.** Go to the **beach** to sit in the sun and swim. Put on sunscreen so that your skin doesn't burn!

Theme parks are full of people having fun! Buy a **ticket** for an exciting ride, and hear people scream. If the theme park is *Dreamworld,* then get ready to enter a world of fantasy! If the theme park is also a **water park,** get ready to get wet!

camping

3 **Work with a partner.** What did you learn? Ask and answer.

4 Listen, read, and sing. TR: B31

If I Went on Vacation

Let's go on vacation!
Let's go on a trip!

If we went on vacation,
we would take a big ship
across the ocean,
far, far away.

If I had my way,
I would go today!

Camping and hiking!
The beach and the sun!
If we went on vacation,
it would be so much fun!

If we went on a tour,
we would see wildlife.
I would take lots of photos.
Wouldn't that be so nice?

CHORUS

I would like to stay at a hotel.
You'd like to relax.

Camping and hiking!
The beach and the sun!
If we went on vacation,
it would be so much fun!

If I weren't afraid of heights,
we could climb a mountain.
But I am! So let's go to the water park
and take pictures by the fountain.

CHORUS

5 **Work with a partner.** Plan a vacation.

1. Where do you want to go? Why?
2. What will you bring with you?
3. What will you do there?

Moremi Game Reserve, Botswana

GRAMMAR TR: B32

If we **went** on a photo safari, I **would take** pictures of lions.
I**'d go** mountain climbing if I **weren't** afraid of heights.
He **wouldn't spend** all of his time in museums if he **didn't like** art.
If you **had** a lot of money, where **would** you **go** on vacation?

6 Read and write.

1. If I ______________ (go) to Egypt, I ______________ (see) the Great Pyramid.
2. If we ______________ (stay) at a hotel near the beach, we ______________ (go swim).
3. She ______________ (go camp) if she ______________ (have) a tent.
4. We ______________ (learn) about the animals in this region if we ______________ (take) an ecotour.
5. If the tour guide ______________ (come) with us, she ______________ (tell) all about this place.
6. If he ______________ (take) the train, he ______________ (see) more of the country.

Tourist train, Victoria, Australia

7 **Work with a partner.** Look at the pictures and make sentences. Take turns.

8 Listen and repeat.

Then read and write. TR: B33

a suitcase

sunglasses

a passport

souvenirs

an airport

1. When you travel to another country, you need a ______________________. It shows who you are and the country where you were born.
2. I always buy ______________________ when I'm on vacation. I like to look at them and remember the fun I had!
3. I don't like to carry a lot of stuff on vacation. I bring a small ______________________ for my clothes.
4. If we arrived at the ______________________ late, we would miss our plane.
5. Has anyone seen my ______________________? The snow is so bright in the sun.

9 **Listen and stick.** Do you think they had a good vacation? Why? TR: B34

1	2	3	4	5

GRAMMAR TR: B35

I **would rather** go on an ecotour than go to a theme park.

We'**d rather** go on a tour than stay at the hotel.
He'**d rather** not eat at that restaurant.

10 **Work with a partner.** Make sentences. Take turns.

1. live by the ocean / in the mountains ______________________

____

2. go camping / stay at a hotel ______________________

____

3. ride a bike on a dirt path / motorcycle ______________________

____

4. walk in the forest / city ______________________

____

5. see wildlife on a photo safari / in the zoo ______________________

____

6. wear sunscreen / get a sunburn ______________________

____

11 **Play a game.** Cut out the board and the pictures on page 173. Choose nine pictures and put them in the spaces. Do not show your pictures. Work with a partner. Take turns.

12 **Listen and read.** TR: B36

Tree House Vacation

Are you ready for a great eco-adventure? Have your vacation in a tree house! You can find them all over the world. Tree house vacations are in places such as Brazil, Kenya, Belize, and India. There's lots to do in nature!

In India, there are tree house bedrooms from 10 to 25 meters (35–80 feet) up a tree. There's a bamboo elevator to carry you up. It's powered by water! The electricity you use comes from the sun. And there are trails to hike and natural swimming pools to swim in. You can visit your neighbor by walking on a bridge made of rope!

You can stay in comfort at a tree house in Kenya. It has two floors, and the rooms have big beds. The windows have colored glass, and the bathrooms have showers. There's a small kitchen, too. The hotel serves food in your room! And if you get tired of living in nature, the city of Nairobi is about 30 minutes away.

In Belize you can live with parrots under a Guanacaste tree that is about 30 meters (100 ft.) tall. The parrots make good neighbors because they eat the insects! There are other birds, too—so it's a great place for bird watching. A river runs around the tree house on three sides. The clear water is good for swimming!

The largest tree house vacation place is in the Amazon in Brazil. There are many tree houses, all connected by more than 8 kilometers (5 mi.) of wood bridges. You can walk through the trees at about 25 meters (65 ft.) high and see the wildlife. Your neighbor may be a monkey!

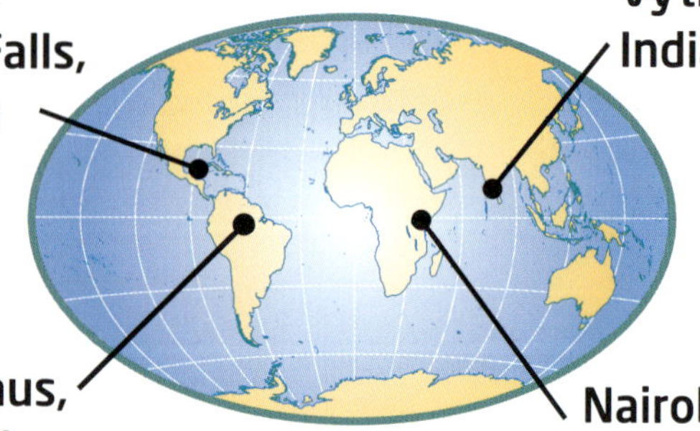

weird but true

A company is planning future vacations on the moon! Some tourists have already visited the space station. But it's expensive!

13 **Where are these tree houses?** Read and write the location.

1. You can live with parrots in a tree house in ______________________.
2. You can vacation in comfort in a tree house in ______________________.
3. The largest tree house vacation place is in ______________________.
4. A bamboo elevator carries you to your tree house in ______________________.

14 **Work with a partner.** Compare places for a tree house vacation. Your partner will listen and complete the first two rows. Then listen to your partner, and fill in the last two rows.

Watching wildlife	
Living in comfort	
Walking on tree bridges	
Using power from nature	

15 **Places for a vacation.** Rank the vacations in order of preference (1 = most favorite). Work with a partner. Compare and explain your choices.

Rank	Vacations	Why you want to go there
	Ice hotel	
	Underwater hotel	
	Sports camp	
	Martial arts camp	
	Make-a-movie camp	
	Astronaut camp	
	Tree house	

Reviews

To make your writing interesting, you can use different kinds of sentences. You can use short, simple sentences to describe your ideas. Or you can combine your ideas into longer sentences. You can also use questions or exclamations.

16 **Read.** Read the ecotour review. Find sentences that describe just one idea, sentences that describe more than one idea, questions, and exclamations.

Review of the Antigua Ecotour

The ecotour in Antigua is a great choice for a vacation. The tour guide takes you to an island and shows you how to paddle a kayak. Then he leads you through a forest of mangroves. The guide knows a lot! He tells you about local fish and the history of the island. The forest is calm and beautiful. It's fun to paddle and not too tiring.

The best part of the tour is the hidden beaches. Why? You can see wildlife, such as pelicans, feeding their young. People wear snorkels as they swim over coral reefs. If you can't swim well, this is hard because the water can be rough. But it's worth the effort because there are amazing, colorful fish to see. If you like water and nature, you should go!

coral reef

stingray

17 **Write.** Write a review of a vacation. Tell what you liked and didn't like. Describe what you saw and did. Remember to use different types of sentences.

18 **Work in a small group.** Share your writing.

NATIONAL GEOGRAPHIC

Mission

Be a respectful tourist.

- Work with a partner. Is tourism always good for a place? How does it help and hurt local people?
- How can tourists show respect for the places they visit? Discuss things you can do and things you shouldn't do. Take notes.

- Share your ideas with another group. Are they the same or different? Decide which ideas everyone thinks are best.

"To bridge cultures you must mix people together. Education and travel are the best teachers."

Joseph Lekuton, Teacher
Emerging Explorer

Vancouver, British Columbia, Canada

19 Make a tourist brochure.

1. Work with a partner. Choose an interesting place in your country.
2. Research the place. What can you do there? What places can you visit?
3. Make a brochure with pictures and text.

Now I can . . .

- ◯ talk about different vacation places.
- ◯ talk about what I would do in different situations.
- ◯ express preferences.
- ◯ write a review.

Review

1 **Read.** Complete these sentences. Use each word only once. Then make similar sentences about yourself.

because of	could	if	when	will	would

1. I couldn't go to the water park __________ the rain.
2. If I have time, I __________ go to the new theme park.
3. A lot of junk __________ be made into art.
4. I __________ run away if a volcano erupted!
5. Some parts of our brain become active __________ we look at art.

2 **Work with a partner.** Talk about your dream vacation.

if / will
if / would
would rather

If my parents say yes, we will go on a photo safari!

I would rather go to a water park!

And if I didn't have to come to school, I would travel around the world for six months.

3 **Work with a partner.** Practice and perform a role-play.

Student A:
You are a scientist who studies volcanoes. Answer the reporter's questions.

Student B:
You are a student interviewing the scientist for the school magazine. Ask questions.

ash	dormant	erupt	extinct	heat	steam
crater	environment	eruption	gas	lava	volcano

Are dormant volcanoes dangerous?

Yes, sometimes they become active.

4 **Work with a partner.** Look at the photo. How can these things be reused?

1. Old cans can be ______________________________.
2. ______________________________
3. ______________________________
4. ______________________________

5 **Listen to the ads.** Check the mini-vacation. TR: B37

	Photo safari	Ecotour
Visit exotic places near your home.		
Get to know your own city.		
Bring a tent and a sleeping bag.		
Make art.		
Get up early on Sunday.		
Bring just a sleeping bag.		
Take pictures at the recycling center.		

6 **Work with a partner.** Ask and answer.

1. What will you do this weekend if you have free time?
2. Of the two weekend tours in activity 5, which would you rather do? Why?
3. If you could travel for six months, where would you go?

7 **Work in small groups.** Create a brochure for a weekend trip near your city.

camping	guide	junk	relax	suitcase	tent	ticket
environment	hike	natural	ruins	sunglasses	theme park	tour

Let's Talk

No way!

I will . . .

- agree and disagree.
- discuss possibilities.
- ask for opinions.

1 **Listen and read.** TR: B38

Maria: Are there any good movies showing tonight, Carla?

Carla: Well, there's a comedy. **What do you think,** guys?

Ivana: **No way!** Comedies are silly. **What else is there?**

Carla: Um, there's an action film. What do you think?

Ivana: Yes! Action films are the best!

Carla: **I suppose so.** But sometimes they are too violent.

Maria: **Exactly!** Isn't there anything else?

What do you think? How about ________?	**No way!** Definitely not! **Exactly!** Right! Totally! Yeah, I agree. Definitely!	**What else is there?** Is(n't) there anything else? Anything else? Do you have any other ideas?	**I suppose so.** I guess so. Maybe. Possibly.

2 **Work in groups of three.** Use the chart. Discuss what to do this weekend.

Our presentation is about . . .

I will . . .
- introduce ourselves.
- explain what our presentation is about.
- check with the audience.
- get started.

3 Listen and read. TR: B39

Gaby: **Hello everyone. I'm Gaby,** and **this is Berto.**

Berto: **Our presentation is about** vacations.

Gaby: **Today we're going to show you** our vacation brochure.

Berto: **Our talk has two parts.** So **I'll start,** and then Gaby **will continue.**

Gaby: **Can everyone see?**

Students: Yes!

Berto: Great. **Let's start.**

Hello (everyone). Good morning. Good afternoon, everyone.	**I'm ________.** **This is ________.** My name's ________. I'd like to present ________.	**Our presentation/ project is about . . .** Our talk compares ________ with ________. **Today we're going to (show you / present)** ________. **Our talk has two parts.**	**Can everyone see/hear?** Can you all see/hear?	**Let's start.** Let's get started. **I'll start/ begin.** ________ **will continue.**

4 Listen. Circle the object that students present in each discussion. TR: B40

1. Mia and Ivan are presenting **a.** a brochure. **b.** an invention. **c.** a poster.
2. Sonia and Juan are presenting **a.** a brochure. **b.** an invention. **c.** a poster.

5 Work in pairs. Prepare and practice presentations.

1. Show the class a brochure you made for your project.
2. Present an invention you created.
3. Show the class a poster you made.

Irregular Verbs

Infinitive	Simple Past	Past Participle
be	was/were	been
beat	beat	beaten
become	became	become
begin	began	begun
bend	bent	bent
bite	bit	bitten
bleed	bled	bled
blow	blew	blown
break	broke	broken
bring	brought	brought
build	built	built
buy	bought	bought
catch	caught	caught
choose	chose	chosen
come	came	come
cost	cost	cost
cut	cut	cut
dig	dug	dug
do	did	done
draw	drew	drawn
drink	drank	drunk
drive	drove	driven
eat	ate	eaten
fall	fell	fallen
feed	fed	fed
feel	felt	felt
fight	fought	fought
find	found	found
fly	flew	flown
forget	forgot	forgotten
forgive	forgave	forgiven
freeze	froze	frozen
get	got	gotten
give	gave	given
go	went	gone
grow	grew	grown
hang	hung	hung
have	had	had
hear	heard	heard
hide	hid	hidden
hit	hit	hit
hold	held	held
hurt	hurt	hurt
keep	kept	kept
know	knew	known
leave	left	left
lend	lent	lent
let	let	let
lie	lay	lain

Infinitive	Simple Past	Past Participle
light	lit	lit
lose	lost	lost
make	made	made
meet	met	met
pay	paid	paid
put	put	put
read	read	read
ride	rode	ridden
ring	rang	rung
rise	rose	risen
run	ran	run
say	said	said
see	saw	seen
sell	sold	sold
send	sent	sent
set	set	set
sew	sewed	sewn
shake	shook	shaken
shine	shone	shone
show	showed	shown
shut	shut	shut
sing	sang	sung
sink	sank	sunk
sit	sat	sat
sleep	slept	slept
slide	slid	slid
speak	spoke	spoken
spend	spent	spent
spin	spun	spun
stand	stood	stood
steal	stole	stolen
stick	stuck	stuck
sting	stung	stung
stink	stank	stunk
sweep	swept	swept
swim	swam	swum
swing	swung	swung
take	took	taken
teach	taught	taught
tear	tore	torn
tell	told	told
think	thought	thought
throw	threw	thrown
understand	understood	understood
wake up	woke up	woken up
wear	wore	worn
win	won	won
write	wrote	written

isn't it?	**is it?**	**aren't they?**	**are they?**
don't they?	**do they?**	**doesn't it?**	**does it?**
were they?	**weren't they?**	**did it?**	**didn't it?**

anyone

everyone

no one

someone

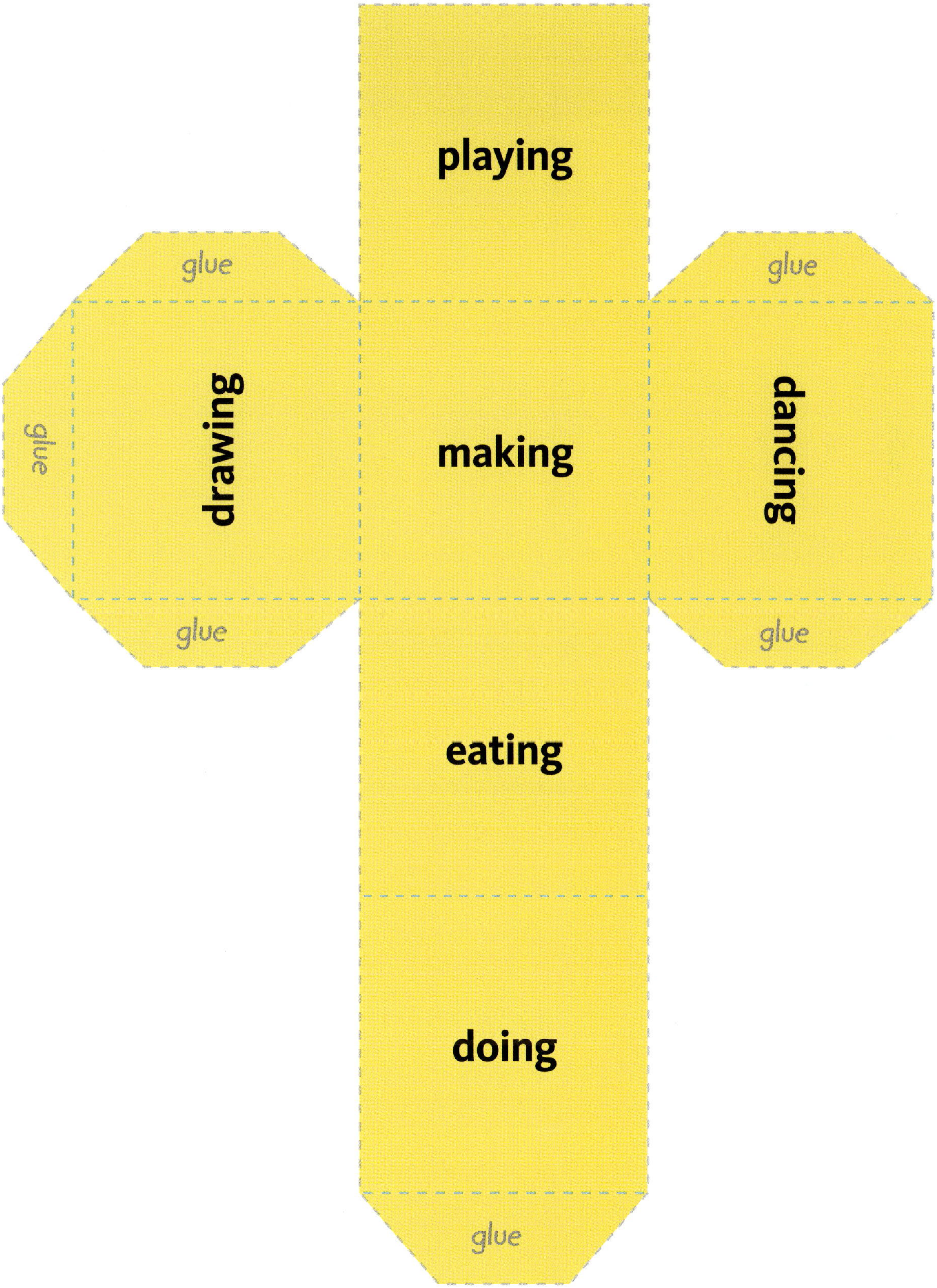
playing
glue
glue
glue
drawing
making
dancing
glue
glue
eating
doing
glue

eruption	cold weather	steam	active volcano
hurricane	ash	lava	heat
rain	snow	sandstorm	tornado
flood	blizzard	heat wave	drought

ECO BAG

	1	2	3
A			
B			
C			

A water park

Horseback riding

Whitewater rafting

Sight seeing

A photo safari

Camping

Playing tennis

Eating in a restaurant

Visiting a science or natural history museum

A visit to an aquarium

Hiking on a mountain trail

A beach

Unit 1
stickers

Unit 2
stickers

TRUE	TRUE	TRUE	TRUE	TRUE
FALSE	FALSE	FALSE	FALSE	FALSE

Unit 3
stickers

Unit 4
stickers

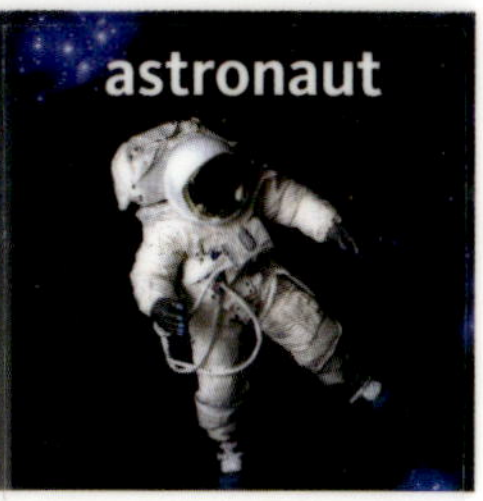

Unit 5 stickers

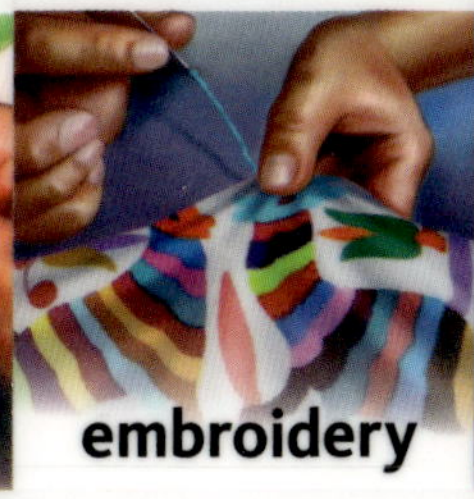

Unit 6 stickers

Unit 7 stickers

active

dormant

extinct

crater

cone

Unit 8 stickers

Unit 9 stickers